MW01223585

WESTERN BARLEY'S LEGACY

The History of the Western Barley Growers Association

1977-2022

Written By

RUSS CRAWFORD

Published by Agrinomics Publishing a division of Agrinomics I.T. Consulting Ltd.

Western Barley's Legacy

Published by Agrinomics Publishing
Creative art work and design by Fiona Farrell Marketing

Cover image provided from the photo archives of Carolyn Otto.
Field images from the farms of Doug and John McBain, Jeff Nielsen and Brian and Carolyn Otto.

This book is an historical account of the activities and accomplishments of the Western Barley Growers Association over their 44 year history, recalled by the people who helped make it happen. Their recollections are based on individual interviews and writings. Any errors or omissions in the text are the responsibility of the author.

ISBN: 978-1-9992805-4-3

DEDICATION

The intention of the founders of the Western Barley Growers Association was to create a greater voice for farmers in Western Canada. These early visionaries, and many more who followed their lead, dedicated themselves to a better livelihood for their communities and for future generations.

This retrospective is dedicated to farmers; to those who earn their living from the land and live their lives with a strong work ethic and a high standard of good human values. In particular, it is dedicated to barley growers and, more specifically, to those who played a part in the organization's endeavours over the past forty-four years.

CONTENTS

WBGA

Foreword

Right Honourable Stephen Harper

Canada's expansive prairie grasslands were originally home to an estimated population of 20,000 to 50,000 Indigenous people, with an economy based on the great buffalo herds. Beginning in the 17th century, British and French fur traders began to trickle into the region. Then, from 1890, there came a much larger wave of immigrants of varied European background. They brought with them a diverse skill set, but farming was by far their dominant occupation. They sought not the rich ore lodes of the American gold rush, but rather, golden waves of ripe wheat, oats, and barley across the massive western plain.

These pioneers entered Western Canada, broke the land for farming, and built a handling and transportation network to deliver their products to world markets. We remember them as settlers or pioneers but, more than that, they were risk-takers. And they were not afraid of hard work to achieve their goals and fulfill their dreams.

Today's prairie farmers, as epitomized by the members of the Western Barley Growers Association, carry on the legacy of their ancestors. In names like Nielsen, Otto, McBain, Robertson, Chatenay, Wagner and Nordstrom, their roots trace directly back to those earliest pioneers of the prairies. They now manage multi-generational, hundred-year-plus family operations and are the keepers of the land for future generations. All Canadians owe them a debt of gratitude for the role they play in producing food and building the Canadian economy in a sustainable manner.

Canada relies heavily on the success and advancement of its agricultural sector. We are blessed to be one of a small number of nations in the world capable of producing more food than we consume, allowing for export-driven economic growth. Our agriculture sector is dynamic, requiring farmers to be innovative, flexible, and persistent. It is also diverse, with different parts of our great country producing a wide variety of products.

As times and conditions change, so too must the practices and policies of agriculture. By the 1990s, when I was first a Member of Parliament for the Reform Party, it had become clear that the future success of Western Canadian agriculture would rest on the dynamism and entrepreneurship of producers. The monopoly of the Canadian

Wheat Board, whatever its original rationale, was rapidly becoming a barrier to the success of a new generation of farmers.

The members of the Western Canadian Barley Growers were always clear to governments in urging greater options for producers. In response, our party led the charge to remove the monopoly. But the battle was long and hard. Members of Parliament from outside rural Western Canada repeatedly blocked the will of farmers in the House of Commons. Still, with the perseverance of the WBGA and other farm groups, the winds of change kept blowing.

The 2011 majority-government victory of Reform's successor, the modern Conservative Party of Canada, broke the impasse. There would be no more partial solutions or half measures. We decided to remove the monopoly completely and let the CWB succeed or fail on its own merits. It was not cheap to extricate the government from the legacy obligations of the CWB but, as I predicted, there would be no going back. Once Marketing Freedom Day — August 1, 2012 — arrived, the defenders of the single desk fell silent, never daring to again raise the issue.

One only need look back on the work accomplished by the WBGA in its 44 years of existence to see the evidence of their positive impact on barley and, in fact, on the entire agriculture industry in Western Canada. Their leadership has been critical. If not for the formation and contribution of the WBGA, Canadian farming would not be what it is today.

Grassroot organizations symbolize the independence and determination of Canada's farm communities. I look back with pride on the results we were able to achieve working closely with this organization, and others like it, who spoke out for the freedom of farmers. The WBGA was always a pleasure to work with, and I congratulate them for their contribution.

Sincerely,

Rt. Hon. Stephen J. Harper
22nd Prime Minister of Canada

Tribute to the WBGA

Contribution by the Honourable Minister Gerry Ritz

Barley ... a Love Hate Relationship

Growing up on a mixed farm, working in all aspects of the farm was a given. To say that work around the farm was always challenging would be a huge understatement. Most memories evoke the enjoyment and satisfaction of doing a job well as part of a self-sufficient family farm team.

On the other hand was the experience of 90 degrees Fahrenheit and an open deck combine with the hopper dust down the back of your neck. Barley! Itchy! Annoying!

I recall the time our family dentist confided in Dad he could tell I had switched from drinking pop to beer. Less cavities. Beer made growing barley worthwhile. However, my Dad took my beer drinking seriously. I remember many hangover mornings being assigned the job of cleaning barley bin bottoms in old buildings cross-rodded every three feet. Suitable punishment I realized when I become a farm father.

Barley was always a mainstay on the grains side of our operation ... six-row varieties as livestock feed and two-row varieties to hopefully ship cars for malt for the beer brewing industry. Of course, at the time, we all played Russian roulette with the Canadian Wheat Board for those sporadic car orders.

We all watched with concern as the government of the day arrested and jailed those folks for simply moving their own product. These actions brought out the worst in government and the best in these "Freedom Fighters" who were vindicated in 2012.

Honourable Minister Gerry Ritz and Jeff Nielsen

Barley continues to come of age as a valuable rotational crop with a growing list of end uses in pet and human consumption. As diverse as the potential uses for barley, were the personalities on the Western Barley Growers Association as they evolved and came of age. As Minister of Agriculture, I had the great pleasure to work for and with many of those men and women and have remained friends with them.

I will not name anyone here. This book does a great job of that. I will simply say "Thank You" to all of them and their families for all they've done and continue to do. You continue to inspire me.

Gerry Ritz

Preface

The history of the Western Barley Growers Association (WBGA) isn't a single event or even a single accomplishment. And it definitely isn't about one or two people. The history of the WBGA is the sum of hundreds of individual contributions and actions from a group of skilled, dedicated farmers. Working alone or in committees, they forged a better agricultural industry for Western Canadian farmers. Looking back on these events and the people who made them happen is an important tribute to their achievements. But rather than recapping a boring, historical summary of the organization, this story is told in the words of the people who blazed those trails and fueled the organization for over four decades.

The history of the WBGA is a compilation of many stories and experiences patched together over time to form something greater, something lasting and functional. As a comparison, the individual squares of a quilt are interesting but not particularly functional on their own but, stitched together, they become a purposeful, valuable treasure that will last a lifetime. A grassroots farm organization like the WBGA is indeed the quilt of the many events in its history.

"WESTERN BARLEY'S LEGACY" is the WBGA's quilt. It's about farmers who combined their skills and energy to produce a body of work that left things better than they found them, a lasting legacy to future generations. It's a compilation of their stories, told in their own words and in the smiles on their faces. "WESTERN BARLEY'S LEGACY" is an invitation to look back with fresh eyes on the dreams and motivations of the original founders of the WBGA and the continuous cast of passionate, noble, dedicated volunteers who carried that torch. Has the end justified the means? That's for you, the reader, to judge.

Acknowledgements

The current board of the Western Barley Growers Association would like to express their immeasurable gratitude to the men and women who contributed their memories of the organization in the compilation of this book. Many industry veterans enjoyed the opportunity to reminisce about people and events that were part of this unique and memorable journey. Their names are listed below and this story is richer, thanks to all of them.

Brenda Brindle
Jay Burrows
Doug Campbell
Colin Carter
Jim Chatenay
Al Constantini
Bob Cuthbert
Phil De Kemp
John De Pape
Art Froehlich
Sheldon Fulton
Glen Goertzen
Jack Gorr
Nithi Govindasamy
Rod Green
Lloyd Groeneveld
Dave Guichon
Stephen Harper
Jim Harriman
Tim Harvey
Mark Hemmes
Alanna Hermanson
Allana Koch
Ike Lanier
Mike Leslie
Blair Louden
Al Loyns
John McBain
Doug McBain
Pat McCarthy
Kim McConnell
Art McElroy
Shelagh McNally
Jeff Nielsen
Richard Nordstrom
Kris Olsen
Paul Orsak
Brian Otto
Charlie Pearson
Richard Phillips
Carman Read
Gerry Ritz
Doug Robertson
Brian Rossnagel
Don Savage
Buck Spencer
Bruce Stephen
Rick Strankman
Bob Sutton
Rick Thiessen
Alberta Wagner

Special thanks are also due to a number of people who contributed to the production of this retrospective work. The people who helped craft the story include the WBGA's Book Committee, Brian Otto, Jeff Nielsen and John McBain, the primary author, Russ Crawford, graphic design and book production, Fiona Farrell Marketing and some dedicated, detailed editing provided by Carman Read, John De Pape and Alex De Pape.

A Note from the Author

In creating this historical saga for the WBGA, I had the extraordinary pleasure of interviewing over 50 veterans of Canadian agriculture and conducting a "deep dive" into the individual memory banks of many unique and interesting people who were the life-blood of the industry and this organization for over forty years. Without exception, every single person was immediately engaged and genuinely thrilled to participate. For many, the conversations often opened a floodgate of memories; recollections of forgotten times and happy thoughts of their days working with others on something meaningful and progressive. The comforting camaraderie within the WBGA was mentioned frequently, along with lifelong friendships forged over countless volunteer hours together, working hard toward common goals.

It was truly an honour for me to interview these wonderful people, to bring the special memories of the WBGA back into their consciousness and capture their fond and heartfelt reminiscences of special times in their past.

For me, these bonds form another square in the WBGA quilt, a square of companionship and empathy for their colleagues. This sense of community is less surprising to people who live a rural life; that's just how they care for and support each other. Every single person who came in contact with the WBGA, its board, its members and its convention gatherings shared similar feelings of pride, success and mutual respect.

Western Barley's Legacy captures an important segment of the history of Western Canada's ever changing and evolving grain industry. The main subject is barley, but there's an underlying theme of the resilience and determination of Canadian farmers. The history of Canadian agriculture is rich with characters and the industry they built. The History of the Western Barley Growers is one of many such stories.

There are a lot of dates and people and places included in the text of Western Barley's Legacy. There's a good chance we didn't get it all right or we omitted some important details, so I'll take the blame for any of those errors or omissions. We have tried to retell the whole story as accurately as possible and do justice to the legacy of the WBGA. Please accept my apologies in advance for any errors or oversights.

Russ Crawford

Part 1

A Call to Action

The chronicles of the Western Barley Growers Association began in Alberta in the mid 1970s. It was a decade of unprecedented prosperity for farmers across North America, brought about primarily by a drought in Eastern Europe, the Soviet Union more specifically. The 70s were turbulent and exciting times for grain markets, combined with emotionally infused political and philosophical differences between farmers. It was also the decade that spawned crop diversification away from traditional cereal grains to new crops like canola and pulses. Prices were sky-rocketing, delivery opportunities were excellent and the future was bright for grain production, with the exception of one crop — barley.

As a traditional rotation crop, well suited for the soil types and climate of Western Canada, barley has always been foundational to prairie farmers. But barley wasn't experiencing the same economic surge as wheat, and barley farmers weren't able to deliver their production to their major buyer, the Canadian Wheat Board, widely referred to simply as the CWB. Not that the CWB traders weren't busy, but they had their hands full selling and shipping wheat in record quantities, leaving barley on the back-burner. In effect, they were preserving barley for the domestic Canadian feed markets in Eastern and Western Canada to consume in traditional amounts, gradually, over the entire year. But that wasn't good enough. At least not for a new progressive, innovative generation of farmers in Western Canada.

Many prairie-based farmers felt the CWB could, and should, be doing a better job on their behalf. They felt an opportunity was being lost. Many of them had lived and farmed through hard times, and knew they needed to make the best of good times because the hard times would be back at some point. And, as the newer, non CWB crops competed for acres and showed the industry another way to market grain, a way that didn't include the single-desk model of the CWB monopoly, many started to question if it was time for a change. They wondered if there was a better way to market barley.

It should be noted that some barley farmers in Western Canada approved of and appreciated the role played by the CWB in marketing their production. A desire for change was not unanimous and it was this divergence of opinion that formed a clear division of views between the two philosophies. So, while some preferred to retain the single-desk marketing approach of the CWB, others began to express a voice for change.

Changes germinate from innovative, open-minded mentalities that thrive on thinking outside the box. A renaissance can begin that way, but in order for it to grow and take shape it needs like-minded collaborators. It takes a special kind of person with vision and perseverance to create long-lasting change.

The entrepreneurial spirit is pervasive across Western Canadian farming communities. People who live a rural life wouldn't have it any other way. It's in their blood. Within these small, geographically separated communities, one or two progressive farmers tend to be local leaders who possess a deeper understanding of their business and a strong vision for its potential. They are often third or fourth generation farmers working the same land as their ancestors for a hundred years. These trend setters innovate and experiment, supporting all that is right and opposing those rules, regulations and practices that are barriers to their success. Some of their neighbours laugh at their outlandish thoughts and actions, while other farmers tend to consider them wise and follow their lead, trusting in their judgement. These community leaders are agents of change, but they often lack peers in their own community who share their vision or drive to innovate, to change. On their own, they are generally unable to tackle major barriers.

Now imagine a collaboration of these grassroots industry leaders, a regional gathering where many of these disparate visionaries connect, communicate and create. They are risk takers with a strong work ethic and commitment to challenge those things that are wrong or unfair and initiate change. At that gathering, a force greater than the sum of its parts is born, a synergy of vision.

Many farms in Western Canada are generational homesteads. They are often managed by second-, third-generation and, in some cases, even fourth and fifth-generations of original pioneers. There is a pride in ownership, an intense devotion to the land and a dream to sustain the family operation for generations to come. Their legacy began with their ancestors and carries on to their children into the future. This is the motivation that fuels these farmers — their families and the land they farm. Their skills are diverse and their dedication unrelenting. They take on all challenges with determination. To underestimate a farmer is to make a grave mistake.

Most people outside the rural community view farmers as independent, self determined, hard-working individuals with a demeanor of quiet acceptance. They are seen to have values that run deep and expect to be treated with fairness, justice and respect, giving the same in return. This is true of most Canadians. That quiet acquiescence washes away however when farmers feel like they are being treated unjustly or unfairly, when they don't get the respect they feel they deserve. Their determination refocuses their resolve on righting a wrong.

Such was the case with farmers who grew barley in Western Canada in the mid 1970s.

Formation

It could be any coffee shop, curling rink or somebody's kitchen where a sharing of ideas and concerns leads to action. These were the traditional gathering places of farmers, places where the conversation ran from a new piece of equipment to the price of grain to the recent passing of a local friend. As distant as people's homesteads are from one another, they make time to get together, to share their lives, their celebrations and their problems. The location is less important than the comradery they share or the current topic of conversation.

In the case of the predicament of the barley markets and the beginnings of what became the WBGA, it began in a small, well-used meeting hall in Carseland, Alberta in 1977. There, a group of "15 or so" like-minded Western Canadian mixed farmers and feeders gathered and formulated a plan to exercise their democratic rights. Out of this meeting came an organization to address their concerns, the Western Barley Growers Association. At the top of their agenda that day was the under-performing feed barley and malt industry and the agency responsible for marketing barley into all export channels and domestic food (malt) channels—the Canadian Wheat Board. Their motivation was survival.

The initial prices set by the CWB and paid to farmers upon delivery were low, delivery quotas were inadequate and shipment of their grain was minimal. CWB management decisions failed to reflect the cash flow needs of the Western Canadian barley farmer and that was a major problem. In addition to the CWB, these farmers were becoming increasingly frustrated with the role of grain companies, who were doing less for more—reduced services at a higher cost. Whenever a new fee or an increase in service costs was introduced into the system the return to the farmer decreased. The outlook for improvement was also not promising: the system in place wasn't working. Something had to be done to stimulate trade and remedy the stagnation.

One of the organization's founders and its first elected president, Lloyd Groeneveld described the group as, "A bunch of dissatisfied farmers who felt we weren't getting a fair shake from the CWB and the grain companies."

The fact that a small agricultural community, thirty minutes south of Calgary, could attract fifteen concerned barley farmers on short notice illustrated how widespread the concerns were in the area. This wasn't even the heart of the barley producing area in Alberta, but the ripple effects were being felt across the province.

"Earlier, in 1974, introduction of an open "non board"[1] market for domestic feed grains had not been enough to offset the price limiting influences of a corn competitive pricing formula, or domestic freight incentives, both designed to keep prices low and support animal feeding outside the prairies. The Canadian Livestock Feed Board was openly opposed to the new domestic market policy, supporting a return to sole marketing by the CWB, a move that worked in their favour thus far. A quote from an early edition of The Barley Growers newsletter summed up the sentiment and building tension and frustration with farmers:

> *"For too many years those with divided loyalties and interests have been influencing policies to the detriment of the barley producer. It is now time that barley is allowed to make its full contribution to the economy of Western Canada and to the livelihood of those who produce it."*

After a second, similarly well attended grower meeting was held in Olds, Alta., a preliminary Board of the newly formed Western Barley Growers Association was established until a formal organizational meeting could be held to elect a representative Board. Richard (Rick) Thiessen, a Strathmore area barley grower and livestock feeder, was selected to act as the Interim President. Rick and his brother Ed managed a mixed farm operation near Strathmore, Alta. growing wheat and barley. They also fed 1,200 head of cattle. "There was no market for barley," recalled Rick. "We had to expand our cattle operations to convert the barley to beef in order to make it work. At the start, barley was so cheap. It was time to make a move."

The tipping point responsible for triggering these conversations had been a recent announcement by the Canadian Grain Commission (CGC) informing the grain industry of an increase in

[1] *Meaning non Canadian Wheat Board.*

country and terminal elevation tariffs without any justification or industry consultation. Who was asking for these increases? And why weren't farmers consulted on handling and storage fee increases? Every single systemic price increase in handling and transportation costs was borne by the farmer. End users wouldn't pay more, so the full weight of these fee increases always came out of the growers' pockets.

An important footnote to the development of the WBGA and other ag commodity groups like the Palliser Wheat Growers and other fledgling farm led associations was the concurrent role of the Alberta government, in particular the Minister of Agriculture and Deputy Premier Hugh Horner. He was a strong believer in empowering farmers to take control of their businesses and supported their lifestyles and desire for independence. It was his belief farm leaders could do a better job than the current CWB monopoly and he opposed greater power to prairie pools in their support of the CWB. Horner's own position of power in the Alberta provincial government gave him the opportunity to influence certain aspects of farm policy. He developed a plan to support the formation of farmer led associations by recruiting a group of intelligent, experienced specialists to work with them alongside provincial and federal legislators to organize themselves and take control of their future. This team of seasoned specialists included Omar Broughton, John Channon and Doug Campbell, all like-minded industry experts with personal records of achievement.

All three of these men ranked prominently in the memories of the members of the WBGA. They are all credited with providing important help and guidance in structuring and expanding the association. These mentors offered on-going support through the early years, addressing numerous issues and providing sage advice and access to decision makers. They stayed below the radar letting the farmers act as the spokespersons and true stakeholders. Without their participation, the success of the WBGA and other farm groups would have taken much longer and perhaps not reached the same degree of success as they managed to achieve. Other government employees followed the path laid out by these forerunners providing a continuous connection to their policy and programs. It's a lengthy list but thanks are due to people like Doug Horner, Shirley McClellan, Ken Beswick, Brenda Brindle, Nithi Govindasamy, Joe Rosario, Dwayne Couldwell, Charlie Pearson, Les Lyster and many more over the years.

> It's important not to lose sight of the role played by Hugh Horner as one looks back on history. It was his vision and his action that paved the way for groups like the WBGA to form and take action. Hugh passed away in 1997. He didn't see all the results of his efforts or the full force and effect of his early initiatives but the industry owes a debt to his contributions.

From the initial formation meetings the association slowly, but steadily, expanded as the founders travelled across the province hosting small meetings in halls and diners trying to drum up support and inform farmers what they were all about. The reception was varied. Lloyd Groeneveld remembers those early meetings, "It was hot and cold; you would go to a meeting and there was a big crowd there and you'd maybe sell two or three memberships," he says. "You'd go to another meeting where there were maybe ten there and you'd sell everyone a membership. We beat the bushes for quite a while and it was frustrating at times. But we managed to get enough to make an organization out of it."

While the spark that lit the fire under this organizing effort was the CGC's announcement of the increases in handling tariffs for all grains, the group always knew they had even larger concerns with respect to the marketing of barley by the CWB. Both of these government agencies had direct impacts on the livelihood of farmers and both of them operated in a vacuum when it came to communicating. There was no transparency or accountability back to the farmer for their actions. There was certainly no form of consulting with farmers in advance of their actions and there was really no mechanism for farmers to voice concerns or offer opinions. Whenever farmers asked questions about marketing or tariffs, the government response was consistent. "Don't worry about it. Let us take care of these things. Just grow the crops and we will take care of marketing them." As if farmers couldn't understand these "complex issues".

The country meetings often turned into philosophical debates between the farmers themselves. Not surprisingly, in areas where the support for the Canadian Wheat Board was strong, the membership sign-up success rate was very low. The WBGA representatives explained they weren't opposed to the CWB. "We weren't fighting the board," Lloyd and others explained, "We just wanted other options. As far as we were concerned, there was no right or wrong side on the debate of single desk selling, just a difference in opinion and philosophy."

Convincing Wheat Board loyalists that their treasured single-desk marketing agency was the problem and not the solution wasn't going to happen in a coffee shop or even after a conference. Loyalties ran deep. Some people might come around, while others were downright militant. So be it, but that's the beauty of living in a free country and having the ability to challenge the government. But first they had to demonstrate they represented a large number of farmers.

In the WBGA's first Press Release in 1977 they wrote:

> "The proposed increases to grain handling and storage tariffs should be discussed with farmers before they are implemented...The Canadian Grain Commission has proposed increases, effective August 1, 1977, of fifty per cent to maximum storage rates at terminal elevators; increases in country elevation charges; and a ten per cent general increase for services provided by the commission... A fifty per cent increase in storage charges just has to be questioned. We don't want companies to make their profit on storing grain, we want them to move it to market."

With a metaphorical "stake in the ground" the WBGA declared their need to be heard.

At the inaugural convention of the WBGA in March 1978, the list of contentious issues grew. Thanks to the input of many concerned barley growers, the Association identified a priority list of urgent concerns affecting the livelihood of their members. When they got into the meat and potatoes of the challenges faced by grain growers in the West, it turned out the list was lengthy. In addition to the proposed tariff changes, they expanded their list of concerns to include transportation such as the Crow Rate and Feed Freight Assistance, producer car availability, declining barley exports, the need for improved price transparency from the CWB, a relatively small portion of research dollars dedicated to barley and overall discontent with the structure of the domestic feed market. The absence of transparency and communication to farmers were at the core of the problem areas. They hadn't even gotten into the larger issues of accountability and an audit of the agencies in place to "protect the farmer". Who was actually watching these appointed agents and overseeing the vital business of marketing their crops?

As the news of the formation of the WBGA spread, farmer discontent became more apparent, the media sensed something interesting was afoot. A Calgary Herald article covering the inaugural convention described the members of the WBGA as a "brash young organization." They were small and largely unknown and what they came to realize was how very little they actually knew about grain markets and the larger commodity industry at home and abroad. According to Rick Thiessen, "We were young and dumb, but the WBGA started to stir the pot. That was the beginning if it." What they lacked in knowledge and experience they made up for in resolve. For them, the status quo wasn't going to meet their needs and if anything was going to change, they were going to have to become more actively involved in making that happen.

A big part of the problem, according to Rick Thiessen, was "How, arbitrarily, a CWB employee decided the export price for barley was too low and wouldn't sell it. Farmers' cash flow requirements weren't considered. The quota system just kept everyone in turmoil. So, when we started poking around, asking questions and providing input, the CWB and CGC reacted to being questioned — they didn't like that."

From inception, the WBGA was disadvantaged to the mighty government controlled Canadian Wheat Board and the Canadian Grain Commission. The farm group didn't have money, power or critical mass to take them on. And they weren't going to get any help from the prairie wheat pools or the other line elevator companies whose profits were dependent on maintaining the status quo. But what they did have was a belief and a vision of a better marketplace, one they would be proud to pass on to future generations. In many farmers' minds the current system could very well bring an end to their operations and even to the existence of family farms. This motivation to change was a powerful offset in this David and Goliath encounter.

It seemed the best word to describe the broader industry reaction to this upstart bunch of activist farmers was "indifferent". This new, unrecognized organization represented a small minority of farmers, they were mostly from Alberta, a well known origin of oppositional thinkers and extremists, and their goals and aspirations were insurmountable in the eyes of the establishment. Initially the grain companies paid the association and their followers little attention and chose not to attend or sponsor their annual conventions but, in a few short years, they witnessed the persistence of the organization and the fact it continued to expand.

Grain companies other than the prairie pools took note of their actions and the developing domestic market. Not all the grain being produced was being delivered to the country elevator system any more. Changes were happening, the domestic industry was evolving and the more trade-oriented companies started paying attention.

Interestingly, grain marketing techniques in the industry were indeed undergoing a structural evolution at the same time the WBGA came on the scene. It was the simultaneous emergence of a timely and unprecedented development in domestic trade, a new breed of grain brokers. In the wake of the recently announced Domestic Feed Grain Policy in 1974, new companies like Palliser Grain and Chinook Grain began appearing on the western scene. They were agile grain marketers providing direct farm-to-feedlot marketing as well as producer car loading to bypass the country elevator system. They offered a new method for farmers to sell grain to them or to act as brokers to existing domestic users. There was a growing discontent with country elevator services and their high elevation costs, grade disputes and lack of delivery space which created an opportunity to fill a gap in service. The grain dealers offered quick, friendly market alternatives and, more importantly, cash flow.

Paul Cassidy, a trader for Palliser Grain in the early years, remembers their market strategy. "We were guerilla traders. We'd pick an area, go after a few target customers and move on to a new area before the big guys knew what happened. We'd attack and retreat. Man that was fun!"

In retrospect, an important synergistic relationship developed between these two groups, as the WBGA and the small grain companies supported each other. The successes of the WBGA might not have been accomplished without the development of these and other small grain dealers who facilitated direct deals, domestic cross-border trade and loading of producer cars. They became a viable alternative to traditional elevator delivery and a harbinger of an evolution in grain marketing in Western Canada.

These companies disrupted the status quo and, together with these progressive farmers, introduced change empowering their peers. According to the President of Palliser Grain, Jim Harriman "We had a young bunch of guys who were eager to make some things happen and a willing client base that wanted change. The fact that so many of those broker/dealer type companies are still around today is a testament to us being in the right place at the right time."

"When the Palliser folks looked at the farmer members of the WBGA and saw the type of people they were dealing with, I think that encouraged them to go ahead with their company," added Lloyd Groeneveld.

Importantly, the grain dealers broke through both bureaucratic and procedural barriers of car loading and fostered forward contracting and interprovincial trade. They by-passed the traditional elevator system for domestic trade, returned more money to farmers and provided important price transparency, all while stimulating trade. Feed grain buyers appreciated them as much as the farmers did. Over time, the larger grain elevator companies pivoted to compete in this direct farm-to-feedlot market, but it was counter to their objective to utilize their elevators for export markets. But, with low delivery quotas and slow movement, more and more barley was moving to non Canadian Wheat Board markets and an economic shift was in the works. The members of the WBGA were already making a difference.

Another Palliser Grain trader, Blair Louden, proudly recalls those days. "I don't know if you would describe the actions of the WBGA farmers and Palliser Grain as disruptive, but they certainly worked together to create change. We were kindred spirits. In the mid 80s the barley farmers we dealt with at Palliser Grain were a forward thinking, proactive group. They were visionary and fearless. It was such a fun time to be working in agriculture."

Initially, the larger grain companies and the CWB viewed the WBGA as a group of inconsequential extremists with some crazy ideas. In reality, these men and women were sensible, reasonable farm operators demanding better service and more control over their businesses. They wanted more say in how their money was spent and they wanted more control over their individual marketing decisions. This was no different than marketing their own production of oilseeds or non CWB feed grains or, importantly, no different than the rights and freedoms of farmers across the rest of Canada outside the Designated Area[2].

"If you don't stand for something, you could fall for anything," WBGA member Glen Goertzen used to tell his kids. Okay, it's a tired, cheesy bit of wisdom, but its relevant. The WBGA needed to define what they stood for if they were going to attract memberships and convince farmers who were on the fence, never mind the 'dyed in the wool' CWB guys. Some would never cross over and abandon their support for the CWB, and that was fine, but maybe they could be convinced to support a dual market approach along

[2] *The Designated Area means that area comprised by the Provinces of Manitoba, Saskatchewan and Alberta, and that part of the Province of British Columbia known as the Peace River District. https://www.canlii.org/en/ca/laws/stat/rsc-1985-c-c-24/latest/rsc-1985-c-c-24.html*

with some of the other crucial topics coming to the surface as the WBGA started investigating.

The agricultural research community was one segment of the barley industry happy to see a group offering a voice for barley. Brian Rossnagel, a plant breeder from the University of Saskatchewan, whose scientific career began in 1977 along with the WBGA, offered his view. "Barley research was an afterthought for Agriculture Canada and the Canadian Wheat Board. Their focus was almost exclusively on wheat research due to the size of the crop and relative value. No money went into feed barley research. What did come barley's way was all for malt varieties." Seed breeders are future-looking people by default. It's the nature of what they do and to finally have a like-minded group sharing their vision added more momentum to a changing barley market.

By the mid 1980s, the WBGA grew to become a vibrant, visionary, action oriented, grassroots organization targeting urgent, important issues with a solution focused approach. They identified inequities and injustice in the Western Canadian agriculture industry and lobbied for positive change based on the broader concept of market freedom. More than just complaining about problems, the WBGA took it upon themselves to consider alternatives and develop solution oriented proposals. In an effort to introduce change and advancement, the WBGA didn't ask "why?" nearly as often as they asked, "why not?"

The WBGA stated its organizational goals and objectives and published them for all to see. It was important for other farmers to understand the drivers of the association. This was their message:

1. To provide a voice that represents the interests of Barley Growers in Western Canada.
2. To hold public meetings to inform and enrol more new members.
3. To issue a regular newsletter to inform members of issues of current interest to Barley Growers.
4. To represent Barley Growers in Legislative matters.
5. To represent Barley Growers' interests to regulatory bodies.
6. To represent Barley Growers concerning transportation issues.
7. Provide liaison with the malt barley trade.
8. To provide liaison with the livestock industry.
9. Participate and advise in the research and breeding of new barley varieties.
10. To investigate and encourage the extension of processing facilities.
11. To encourage marketing alternatives for Western Barley Producers.

It should be noted the eleven goals were, essentially, the scope and responsibility of the CWB as the sole marketer of all barley grown in Western Canada. So why was there a need for the WBGA at all? The simple answer in the minds of its founders was the CWB wasn't doing its job—at least not to the satisfaction of many hard working farmers it was supposed to serve.

In a strategic and collaborative effort, the members of the WBGA began to get involved in other influential groups. They joined other association's committees, got representatives elected to their boards and secured appointments to provincial and national committees developing policies and programs that affected their livelihoods. They lobbied for causes they believed were important to farmers and became influencers before that was even a thing.

Over the years, the WBGA took the lead on many important issues which will be shared here through the personal experiences of many participants. Throughout the 1980s the WBGA lobbied hard for an open dual market for grain, a Voluntary CWB. They also lobbied for cost-effective transportation — not just least cost, effective Crop Insurance and Risk Management mechanisms, and for the payment of the Crow Benefit to the farmer rather than the railways.

Source: WBGA historical files

Another major thrust of the association was to educate farmers about how their own grain marketing system worked. As well as lobbying on behalf of the farmer, the WBGA educated them about their own industry, providing ways to improve their individual farms' bottom lines. Through farmer training and well researched and written monthly market analysis reports and annual magazines, the WBGA filled a void of market information to help farmers make better marketing choices. They set up annual summer seminars and producer forums and meetings that helped farmers understand how markets worked so they could begin their own process of self-determination. They peeled back the layers of bureaucracy and complexity to get to the heart of meanings, pros and cons and the impact on farmers.

From their monthly newsletter...

As well as lobbying on farmer's behalf, the WBGA has done its best to continue to educate farmers about their own industry, providing ways to improve their farm's bottom line. One of our most popular ongoing workshops has been the Roy Ferguson Seminars. Each year we also host one of the most informative and dynamic annual conventions in agriculture, with speakers from the top of their field in agribusiness, weather, markets, and all facets of agriculture. Throughout the year we often have seminars and information sessions designed to help farmers take control of their own industry as well.

The Western Barley Growers Association believes that only an informed farmer, who understands how their industry really works, can take control of their own future in agriculture. Farmers deserve to benefit fully from their own hard work. We can no longer afford to carry those who add no value to our farms on our backs, especially without fair compensation.

While the WBGA is probably best remembered for the role they played in the ultimate removal of the CWB monopoly, they did more for farmers, a lot more. Their history is a look back at the initiatives they addressed and the people who led the charge for change across a wide range of farm related topics.

The forty-four year story of the Western Barley Growers Association is filled with memorable people, places and events. The WBGA carved out a place in Canadian agricultural history, not for credit or recognition but simply for the benefit of all farmers. Their journey starts here.

Who Speaks For Barley?

Initially, an organization starts out as an idea. In due course it acquires a name, some goals and maybe even a mission statement. What determines its value and efficacy are the people who come together to work on behalf of those goals. Year after year WBGA attracted countless volunteers and stellar leadership from many insightful, well spoken members. The association quickly developed a reputation of vision, integrity and a positive approach to their messages. Its leaders and members took the high ground, never advocating the dismantling of institutions but, rather, their improvement. The WBGA Board and committees were represented by many intelligent, dedicated farmers who collectively "punched well over their weight class" against formidable opposition and unfair regulations. Agriculture will forever be indebted to them. The stories and insights of many of these heroes are shared in the pages that follow.

It's impossible to spotlight every single person who contributed to the growth and success of the WBGA since it's inception. But several people distinguished themselves among their peers and were mentioned often by the contributors to this book. The frequent recollection of these exceptional people merits mentioning their contributions specifically.

Gordon Reid

In the early years of the association's development, the WBGA benefited from the wisdom and clarity of Gordon Reid. His well written articles and stalwart leadership laid a foundation for the development of priorities and policy platforms utilized by the WBGA over the years. In the June 1983 edition of the WBGA newsletter one of Gordon's articles, *"Who Speaks for Barley?"* succinctly defined the genesis of the WBGA. Not so much in the content of the article itself but, rather, in the nature and direction of the title. The truth was, no one spoke for barley, not the CWB, not the government, not the prairie pools or grain companies and not the livestock industry. No one was focused on the best interests of barley farmers. Gordon was crystal clear in his messaging — barley growers would have to speak for themselves.

Gordon Reid was born and raised on a century old family farm in Cremona, Alta. He was a founding member, former president and director of the Western Barley Growers Association from 1977 until his passing on April 18, 2014. After 36 years of persistent work, he saw Western Canadian grain growers freed from the monopoly of the CWB and, with a great sense of accomplishment for his country, enjoyed Market Freedom Day on August 1, 2012.

Looking back at some of his articles we see his style of plain speaking and a direct approach. With his wisdom and experience it isn't a stretch to describe Reid as the Yoda[3] of the WBGA. In an

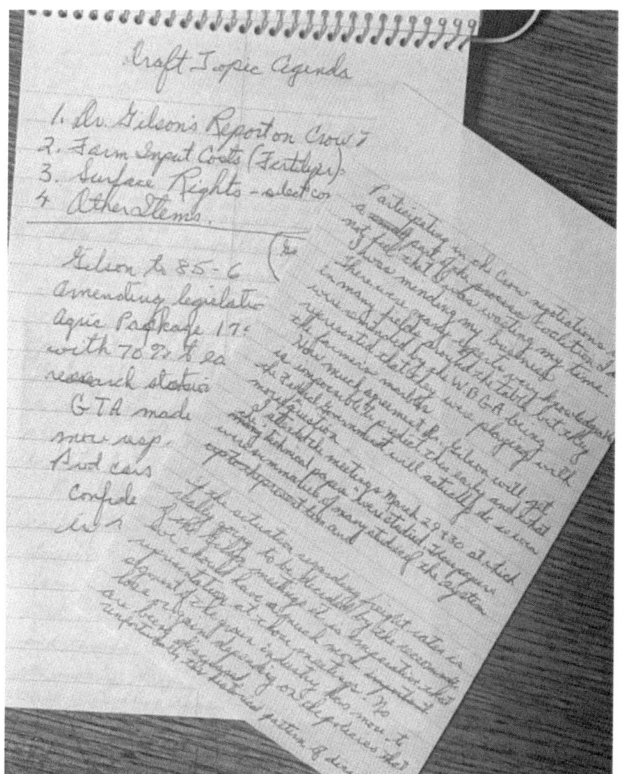

Draft Topic Agenda

1. Dr. Gilson's Report on Crow
2. Farm Input Costs (Fertilizer)
3. Surface Rights
4. Other Items.

[3] *If this isn't familiar see "Star Wars" characters but, seriously, where have you been?*

article published in the Western Producer in 2008, he offered these thoughts. "I have a long history of not wanting too much government interference. I was not happy when they instituted the monopoly on barley, which is our main crop here, in 1948. I have seen a lot of changes and about 90 percent of them, I have been against," he said, laughing.

During Gordon's years as a barley grower, member, President and Past President of the WBGA he continually lobbied for change. His weapon of choice—the pen. He took copious notes, summarized his thoughts and craftily presented them in a clear and understandable manner.

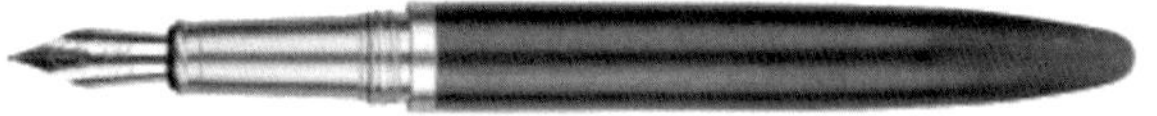

Without the voice of the WBGA, many programs and regulations may have been structured to the detriment of barley growers. For example, Gordon wrote on the faults of the Market Assurance Plan as an ill conceived scheme to use farmers' money to "buy and store surplus production thereby creating additional cost and bureaucracy." He railed at attempts by the CWB to regain control over domestic feed markets, pointing out their ongoing failure to expand export barley markets in favour of wheat trade. This had resulted in low quotas and poor initial and final payments for barley. He called the Board's plan "economic serfdom" and chastised the prairie wheat pools for suggesting the maintenance of strong producer support for total CWB control. That simply wasn't true and he called out the pools for making an erroneous statement.

The federal government was not immune to Gordon's program and policy scrutiny or the skewer of his pen. From a flawed Liberal government proposal to change capital gains taxes in 1981, to a scheme developed by governments to create a minimum price for wheat, to the contentious debate over removal of the Crow Rate and the subsequent payment benefits, Gordon challenged all who opposed benefits to farmers. He was particularly incensed by Senator Hazen Argue, the Minister of the Canadian Wheat Board. In the 1983/84 crop year, Senator Argue indicated a desire on the part of the federal government to hold back export sales of barley as part of the development strategy of an international grain cartel. This declaration of nonsense came on the heels of two consecutive annual drops in the initial price paid for barley by $.30 per bushel or more.

Gordon was an ardent supporter of open markets stemming from price transparency and free market price discovery. He also advocated for competition in all its forms to deliver the best signals and returns for farmers. On this topic he wrote:

> *"The concept that ONE grain company, ONE railroad, and ONE marketing agency will deliver the farmer the most return is a myth. The grain system should be a balance between cost effective efficiencies on one hand and competitive pricing and service performance on the other. Competition is the lever that pries the profits of technological improvements and operating efficiencies from the system and makes them available to the farmer."*

Take a second and read that last paragraph a second time. It's powerful insight.

This viewpoint was passionately and uniformly shared by fellow members of the WBGA, providing a clear vision of the organization's raison d'être. The subsequent development of a Dual Market Proposal by the WBGA was a key deliverable of the association stemming from this view. It proposed market choice in addition to the single desk alternative — competition that was sorely lacking.

Gordon lobbied the Canadian Grain Commission for producer rights to load their own cars and worked closely with friend and fellow WBGA Director, Cal Ausenhus in delivering the association's position. He supported any initiative to develop a strong, prairie based livestock feeding industry and opposed the systemic bias that favoured larger grain companies over smaller, innovative businesses. He encouraged more active farmer participation in the democratic process of electing pool delegates.

Who speaks for barley?

Gordon Reid epitomized the driving force of the dedicated founders, the present and future members of the WBGA. He spoke solemnly and passionately for barley throughout his lifetime. He was widely respected inside and outside the association as a serious leader and agent for change. He, for one, spoke for barley.

Omar Broughton

Simply put, the WBGA would likely not exist without the advice and guidance of Omar Broughton. Empowered by then Alberta Agricultural Minister Hugh Horner, Broughton acted in his capacity as "Marketing Commissioner" for Alberta Agriculture to help organize and connect a confused, uncertain group of barley farmers into a respectable commodity organization. He did this for other commodity groups such as beekeepers and goat owners. Broughton and Horner shared a vision of strong, independent farmer-led commodity organizations speaking on behalf of their industry to drive change and advance their individual sectors. He was attracted to groups that would do things for themselves, rather than wait for government agencies or agricultural companies to act.

Doug Robertson, president of the WBGA, expressed gratitude for Broughton's guidance in the early days. He recalled some words of encouragement Broughton received from Minister Horner and shared with the WBGA. "Hugh used to say that the problem with politicians and bureaucrats is they didn't want to solve problems for fear they would work themselves out of a job. He told me, Omar — go out and solve this problem. I have lots more for you to work on. So that gave me all the permission I needed to help farm groups like the barley growers get established." Omar said he liked Horner a lot more after that conversation because he was so supportive. Robertson also recalled, "Omar never took credit for anything he did for us. He just wanted us to succeed."

After serving in the Second World War as an RCAF navigator on the Sunderland Flying Boats off the coast of Scotland and North Africa, Omar returned to get a B.Sc. at the University of Alberta. Degree in hand, he returned to farming but developed other interests such as a radio announcer with CJOC in Lethbridge. He later joined the Alberta Wheat Pool (AWP) in 1957 as their Corporate Secretary and Executive Assistant to the President. At AWP, Omar developed many industry contacts through his position and learned the grain business from inside one of the major provincial players. His good friend Gordon Reid quipped "working with the AWP gave Omar an idea of what he didn't want for farmers!"

Broughton didn't confine his attention to Alberta groups either. In the early days of the Saskatchewan-based producer organization, the Palliser Wheat Growers, he accompanied them on a trip to Winnipeg to visit the Canadian Wheat Board. As he told it, the CWB really didn't know what to do with a group of farmers who invaded the Winnipeg fortress of the CWB. They were appalled with the farmers' forthright approach and their challenging questions and suggested "These people should just trust that we know what's best for them."

Broughton played a key role in the founding meeting of the WBGA's organization in Blackie. Lloyd Groeneveld credited Broughton as being very instrumental to the early set-up of the WBGA. Southern Alberta farmer Ike Lanier added, "He helped us on the side, mostly on his own time. He really helped us get organized. He was like the local sheriff and very supportive of the WBGA."

In the weeks and months that followed those founding sessions, Broughton coached the barley growers from the sidelines as he set up key meetings with bureaucrats and counselled the farmers in setting up the organization. He continued to provide moral support and a good sounding board for numerous challenges as they arose, maintaining a membership in the organization right up to his death in 1997. He and his wife Anne moved back to a farm near High River in 1983 and he was presented with an Honorary Lifetime Membership to the WBGA for his unparalleled service to the organization over the years.

Another long-time member of the WBGA, Viking area farmer Richard Nordstrom, knew Broughton well and wanted to see him achieve the recognition he deserved. "We tried to get him accepted into the Alberta Agriculture Hall of Fame on three occasions without success," he said. When they told Broughton about their unsuccessful efforts Omar replied dryly, "Well there are still a few people there in the government I tramped on pretty hard. There may still be some bad feelings." But he had no regrets.

This "true gentleman" of agriculture was an industry icon with a soft spot in his heart for farmers. He dedicated has latter years to volunteering to preserve Alberta's agricultural heritage and will always be remembered as a true friend of the WBGA.

Lloyd Groeneveld provided this insight on Omar Broughton's commitment to the WBGA:

"To see this organization alive and well today means those efforts were not in vain. Many sincere and dedicated people helped build this organization and I hesitate to name names in case I miss someone, but we cannot talk about the history of this organization without mentioning Omar Broughton. He is not with us today but his quiet tenacity, his political savvy and his sincere desire to see the grower get a fair shake kept us inspired and helped this association grow to what it is today."

John Channon

A heartfelt tribute to another Alberta government employee who championed the development of the WBGA goes to John Channon. John had a lust for learning and a spirit to fight injustice. He was very humble and the consummate professional. When you spoke with John you knew you had his undivided attention and you knew he was really listening to what you had to say. Born in Montreal and educated at McGill, he seemed right at home in Alberta. Channon's character was a perfect fit for the West and he delighted in working with the entrepreneurs and "radical farm groups" here.

Channon came to Alberta to become the first chairman of the Alberta Grain Commission in 1972. He came from Ottawa with a wealth of experience in grain transportation, Statistics Canada and as a ministerial advisor. He was known to favour the farmer and did whatever he could to make sure farmers had at least as much information in their hands as the bureaucrats.

Hugh Horner liked that characteristic and recruited the charismatic Channon to come to Alberta. John was quick to embrace the fledgling farm groups and worked diligently in helping them get stronger and spread their message. He had some strong feelings on the CWB too. He believed the CWB had far less power when it was formed than it did at the present time. In his view they were vulnerable to court challenges on their authority and wondered why no one had actually taken them to court over their stand on various issues. The Alberta Barley Commission and WBGA Charter Challenge, launched in 1993, brought a smile to his face. John Channon passed away in 1996 at the age of 78.

Cal Ausenhus

One other individual was remembered by many as they thought back on the history and highlights of the WBGA. Cal Ausenhus had been a friend to all and an innovator in grain marketing outside the bounds of the CWB. Cal was one of the first people to load producer cars in Alberta. Not afraid of a little extra work to load his own cars, he quickly attracted the interest of others who wanted to do the same. What started out as helping a few friends, turned into a business for Cal when more and more farmers reached out to him for help. In 1979 Cal and some partners started Chinook Grain which offered producer car loading services and a saving of approximately $.25 per bushel to farmers. He knew he was on the right track when local elevator agents started a negative ad campaign against him. The ultimate moment came when one elevator agent called him directly demanding he charge $.25 per bushel more for his services because the agent was losing business. His pioneering efforts as an independent grain dealer helped revolutionize commodity trading on the prairies.

Cal loved the idea of the WBGA and joined immediately and actively recruited more members.

He became close friends with neighbour Gordon Reid and this led to a sharing of ideas and projects advocating farmer rights. Cal was a champion for all farmers. He was involved in the development of other producer groups, the Western Barley Futures contract and eventually sat on the Winnipeg Commodity Exchange as a Governor.

Cal was inducted into the Alberta Agriculture Hall of Fame posthumously in 2000. He passed away at a young age in a vehicle accident in 1997. The attendance of more than 1000 people at his funeral service in Didsbury during harvest spoke to the number of friends he had in his life.

Agriculture Industry Champions

These individuals are but a few of the many contributors who championed the cause of barley in Western Canada. In the following pages many more people will be acknowledged. Its important to recognize these types of efforts were not confined to barley. Over the years many champions of Canadian crops emerged, people like James McAnsh for canola in the early 1970s and Gord Bacon for special crops and pulses in the 1980s and 90s. The champions for wheat are too many to name just one or two individually, but the WCWGA history books acknowledge all of their efforts very well. Many more people dedicated their efforts to improving Canadian agriculture and this brief volume recognizes a few of them.

The WBGA, as an organization, had a life of its own as the longest continually running farmer managed commodity group in Canada, starting in 1977 and continuing to this day, nearly 45 years later. The WBGA is a testament to Western Canadian farmers' belief, dedication and tenacity. Every single person who touched this association in some way, big or small, contributed to its success. A tip of the hat to you all!

The Canadian Wheat Board

Source: https://globalnews.ca/news/1939906/canadian-wheat-board-sold-to-saudi-owned-global-grain-group/

This book isn't about the Canadian Wheat Board. But looking at the history of the WBGA without including the parallel events and interactions with the CWB would leave out a great deal of the story. The history of the CWB is another book (or maybe two) involving layers of complexity and a classic case study investigation into corporate governance. The story of the CWB's ability to survive, reinvent itself, gain power and garner support from politicians and farmers is unlike any other business review. However, the interplay between the CWB and farm groups like the WBGA is most definitely part of this story.

The conflict between the bureaucratic, political powerhouse Canadian Wheat Board and the small but mighty farmer group was epic. The CWB operated under a legislative act known as the Canadian Wheat Board Act. This gave the CWB unbalanced power over the very farmers it was legislated to serve. Long after the CWB fulfilled its Wartime Measures obligations to support the provision of food to Allied Forces during World War II, it persisted as a government bureaucracy. It proclaimed to speak for the farmers of Western Canada, but when any farmers opposed its actions or challenged the performance of the CWB, they denied any malpractice, defended themselves vigorously — and paid for that defence with the farmers' money!

"The CWB thought they were spokespersons for barley, but they weren't," stated WBGA member and director and past president Brian Otto.

Some farmers supported the role and responsibilities of the CWB, believing the agency protected their interests against unscrupulous buyers. They believed the CWB was able to extract premiums from international buyers as the exclusive seller of cereal grains[4]. And they liked the fact everyone received the same price and delivery options regardless of location or farm size. Many farmers ardently supported the co-operative movement of the prairie wheat pools and their single desk agent, the CWB. But other farmers felt they could do a better job of marketing their own grain. They wanted more freedom in their marketing choices and timing of sales than those provided through the CWB monopoly. They felt constricted by delivery quotas and small initial payments and they had a growing sense the CWB wasn't being totally honest with farmers. There was no transparency or accountability for the CWB's actions, resulting in a building suspicion and lack of satisfaction in the CWB's performance. The fact the CWB would refuse to respond to specific questions nor provide requested transparency added to the growing suspicion and mistrust. This polarity of beliefs created two distinct opposing groups. For farmers, there was black and there was white, there was no gray area on this matter.

Farmers who opposed the market monopoly of the CWB were frustrated by low grain movement and disappointing cash returns from CWB sales. In frustration, many farmers shifted their crop choices away from cereal grains to other crops such as rapeseed (now canola), flax and various specialty crops. These farmers discovered and developed their own abilities to market their grain production and deal directly with independent buyers. They wanted that same ability to market their traditional cereal grain crops (wheat, durum, oats and barley).

Politicians, past and present, also had diametric views in regard to the CWB. Some saw it as a way to pander to eastern voters with distorted, low feed grain prices, while others tried, in vain, to make change. Left and right leaning political lines were drawn—with the odd exception—leaving farmers adrift in the middle without a paddle and more than a few leaks in their boat.

[4] *Numerous studies and analytical reviews proved without question this claim was false. In fact the CWB continuously achieved sub average returns in comparison to market values.*

Modern day Liberals of the 1980s and 1990s were united in their support of the CWB. You have to look back to the 1960s to find a Liberal voice who felt differently. Mitchell Sharp, best remembered as one of the most unpolitical of politicians, was a Liberal cabinet minister under both Pierre Trudeau and Lester Pearson. He shared his insights on the CWB in his 1994 memoirs[5].

> "Canada's government had committed wheat sales to Britain at an artificially low price and wanted to shift the burden to farmers. Against the wishes of Canada's Minister of Agriculture, the CWB got its monopoly and squeezed prices down. Fifty years later, the "temporary monopoly" still exists. "Choice" advocates did not propose to eliminate the CWB, but rather, end its legal buying monopoly."

Sharp's comments predated the actions taken in 1977 by Western Canadian barley farmers but they identified the same flaws the organization opposed more than a decade later.

After World War II, farmer support for the CWB hinged on three premises; i) a sense of protection from those "unscrupulous grain brokers", ii) a lack of understanding of grain markets and iii) a belief that a single-desk selling agency could capture "market power" premiums from international customers while protecting the domestic feeding industry. Massive wheat deals with countries like the Soviet Union and China seemed to corroborate claims the CWB monopoly was beneficial to farmers. But without checks and balances, and any accountability to farmers or political leaders, there was no way to know. The CWB was not subject to audit by the government, so even they didn't fully know what was going on from either a financial accounting or a business decision perspective.

As every farmer knows, barley and oats[6] were also controlled by the CWB in addition to wheat. (the Canadian "Wheat" Board almost seems like a misnomer). The same temporary measures status applying to wheat sales also applied to export feed barley and export and domestic malt barley. But this "one size fits all" approach wasn't working for all barley farmers.

In 1989, thanks to persistent efforts by the WBGA and other like-minded groups, Charlie Mayer, then Federal Minister of Agriculture, removed oats from the monopoly control of the CWB. Barley was to be next on his list. Since the removal of oats, an open market has developed, transforming the crop from a light-weight horse feed to a grain that is much higher in quality, now recognized globally for its superior characteristics as a race horse feed. It's also more widely used as human food and fractionation techniques continue to show promise for the future.

---

[5] *A quote from the November 15, 1996 Wall Street Journal article by David Henderson referring to "Which Reminds Me... A Memoir" by Mitchell Sharp, University of Toronto Press.*

[6] *Oats until 1989.*

Unfortunately, Mayer failed to set out the same freedom for barley during his tenure as minister, thinking he still had time to get that done during his appointment. His attempt to develop more open trading by way of introducing the Continental Market in August 1993 was a disappointing failure (more on this to come) and the subsequent federal election loss of the Conservative government three months later eliminated the chance for any further liberalization of trade — because the Liberals won. There is certainly irony in that — Liberals/liberalization.

Ample support for more deregulation of grains came from the Conservative Party, mostly from Western Canada. However, the governing Liberals, following Ralph Goodale's lead as Minister of Agriculture and Agri-Food, were staunchly opposed to any changes that would alter the power and exclusivity of the CWB. With the Liberals regaining the federal leadership in 1993, they effectively halted any effort to change along with the developed momentum (such as the Continental Barley Market). The right-wing parties were in shambles for more than a decade following the change in government in 1993 as their identity shifted from Progressive Conservative, to Reform, to Canadian Alliance, to the rebirth of the Conservative Party in 2006. During that whole period, the WBGA lacked effective, actionable political support for their goals.

Regardless of the government in power, the position and messaging of the WBGA towards the CWB remained consistent. From their foundational beginning, the WBGA promoted more open, transparent markets. They were advocates of a dual market, never suggesting an end to the CWB. Time and time again, it was the CWB who proclaimed a dual market option was impossible (for them at least), so farmers had to accept the status quo. Any discussion on change was restricted to the comparison of the single-desk option that had served them since the late 1930s or an open market without the CWB. No middle ground. The CWB fostered the image of sharks in the water circling the CWB boat. You're "safe" as long as you stay on board.

One of the more widely known and respected farm voices of the time was Jack Gorr, a farmer from Three Hills, Alta. Gorr was a twenty-two year veteran of the Alberta Grain Commission and a Director for both the Wheat and Barley Grower Associations. His views on the CWB aligned with those of both organizations. However, his insight on the impact of the CWB on the agriculture industry in Western Canada sheds a different light on the widely disputed sides for, and against, the government agency.

"I wasn't a hater of the Board but I could see where it really interfered with all the companies trying to manage their own inventories, sales and exports," says Gorr. He goes on to add, "The CWB system didn't really accommodate an individual farmer."

The truth was, the CWB didn't really understand the feed barley market. "They never were marketers. They were regulators," says Buck Spencer. They prioritized malt as a premium crop and welcomed the large volume purchases of the individual malting companies. They also gravitated to the large export feed barley trades to several key international destinations. The North American feed industry was too pedestrian for them. It involved small volumes, low prices and an exceptional amount of logistics, shipping, tracking and accounting for single truck lots. They didn't want to do it, but they also didn't want to allow anyone else to do it, at least outside the borders of Canada. This was likely viewed by CWB management as the "thin edge of the wedge" that could work against their greater goal of exclusivity, so the simple solution was to just forbid any direct dealings.

In the early 1990s, winds of change blew through the halls of the CWB at 423 Main Street in Winnipeg. The Board of Directors of the CWB encouraged the organization to consider modernizing the sixty-year old agency as the marketplace around them evolved. In a Journal Article[7] published by Grace Skogstad in 2005 she eloquently described the circumstances:

> *"...individuals within the Wheat Board recognized the shifting terrain in which the organization functioned. Its marketing function kept Wheat Board officials in regular contact with grain farmers. They became fully aware of its diminishing reputation among young farmers who were willing to assume more individual responsibility and risk for their own grain marketing. Convinced the Wheat Board needed to adapt in order to survive, mid-level officials persuaded their leadership to appoint the Canadian Wheat Board Review Panel (1990) to examine the role of the Board in prairie grain marketing. Following its report the Wheat Board galvanized around two changes in particular. The first called for the Board to become more democratic and more accountable to prairie farmers. Replacing government-appointed commissioners with fairer-elected commissioners was proposed as a way to give farmers "an effective voice and sense of ownership" in the board and more direct say in its operations (Hehn, 1997). The second set of changes was ultimately more controversial because it appeared to jeopardize one of the institution's core ideational principles. It proposed giving farmers more pricing options by adding the option of cash pricing to pool pricing. Cash pricing would allow the Wheat Board to offer farmers a cash payment in place of the pooled price to induce grain shipments when Wheat Board inventories were inadequate to meet customers' demand. Critics worried that if the option of cash pricing were used routinely by the board, farmers would have an incentive to hold their grain on the farm until the market was short and the Wheat Board was forced to offer a cash payment higher than the pooled price. Price pooling would soon disappear as an attractive option."*

7 *Skogstad, Grace. "The Dynamics of Institutional Transformation: The Case of the Canadian Wheat Board." Canadian Journal of Political Science / Revue Canadienne de Science Politique, vol. 38, no. 3, Canadian Political Science Association, 2005, pp. 529–48, http://www.jstor.org/stable/25165842.*

In response to recommendations from the CWB Board of Directors to modernize, federal Agriculture Minister, Ralph Goodale hand-picked a nine member Western Grain Marketing Panel in 1995. Following directions from Goodale, they executed their mandate by holding public meetings and gathering feedback. Despite the panel members' professional roots and bias towards the CWB and prairie pools, they returned with a report that advocated partial deregulation and freedom for Western farmers to sell their exports of feed barley to any buyer, not just the CWB. At the same time, the Alberta government held their own vote among farmers on whether they wanted to maintain the CWB monopoly over the export sale of prairie wheat and barley with a similar response. That vote resulted in a margin of 2-1 for free trade. Later that year, a confidential poll by Ag Canada was leaked to the Toronto media. It showed 55% of prairie farmers supported the ending of the CWB monopoly on barley. Three separate reports revealed the message was clear — but the minister chose not to listen.

An important outcome from this process was the WBGA refortified their allegiance with the Alberta provincial government. In addition to their survey, the government's agriculture Ministry became more active in lobbying Ottawa and supporting investigative analysis into the claims made by the CWB. One such action the government of Alberta took in moving the dial on the monopoly rhetoric was to commission a study entitled The Economics of Single Desk Selling of Western Canadian Grain[8]. Colin Carter and Al Loyns were two highly-regarded research analysts who collaborated on the study reviewing many aspects of single-desk performance in Canada and Australia, the Continental Market experience and the CWB. Their study mandate stipulated they consider the benefits and costs of single-desk selling, not the elimination of the CWB. Their findings, submitted in March 1996, offered substantiated evidence on the costs and efficacy of single-desk selling versus open markets.

The conclusions in the section on "Costs of the Single Desk Buyer and Seller" were particularly persuasive:

- "There is a sub-optimal allocation of resource in prairie agriculture and CWB regulation is one of the contributors because it interferes with farm-level decision making and the grain handling system.
- The creation of more efficient markets would lead to improved incentives for profit maximization, efficiency gains and higher incomes throughout the system.
- The average yearly cost of the single desk in wheat is at least $20/metric tonne to the farmer and an additional $5.00/metric tonne to the taxpayer. **In the case of barley, the figures are slightly higher**.

[8] *"The Economics of Single Desk Selling of Western Canadian Grain", Colin A. Carter and R.M.A Loyns March 1996.*

- All of our cost estimates are considered to be very conservative in level and we have not been able to measure a significant number of additional costs.
- In its present single desk form, the CWB contributes significantly to inefficiencies and costs in the Canadian grain system."

The results confirmed the views and public stance of the WBGA and provided impetus for them to continue to lobby for an end to the CWB monopoly.

Colin Carter shared a retrospective of his work studying grain marketing in Canada since the early 1970s. "I started looking at the marketing efficiencies of a dual market versus the single desk when I first came to Winnipeg in the early seventies. Even then it was clear to me there was a better way for markets to function and improve returns to farmers, an important topic to me with my own farm background in Sexsmith. It was an obvious fact the CWB affected all aspects of the Canadian grain market, not just wheat, oats and barley. They influenced the movement, storage and marketing of all crops either directly or indirectly."

"In my research and travels," Carter continued, "I spoke with customers and potential customers of Canadian grains and compared marketing systems. For instance, the U.S. malting companies and feeders wanted the opportunity to buy Canadian barley, but the CWB wasn't interested in talking to them. Our research[9] for Agriculture Minister Charlie Mayer led to the brief opening of the Continental Market. I also learned, what the CWB was saying publicly to farmers and what they were actually doing (for customers) was very different."

After two short decades (yes, that's sarcasm), the efforts of the WBGA were finally creating change. It's unlikely anyone imagined it would take this long and equally surprising that the farmers' perseverance for marketing freedom continued. But that's what happens when you get a Canadian farmer riled up.

Accepting the two recommendations for expanded governance structures and more flexible pricing options, Minister Goodale introduced legislation in December 1996 to amend the Canadian Wheat Board Act. Prior to these changes, five appointed commissioners acted as its board of directors. It was replaced with a fifteen member board made up of five appointees and ten elected farmers. Rather than accept the findings of his own panel on partial deregulation, Minister Goodale opted to conduct a plebiscite in 1997 where farmers were asked to decide between a continued CWB single desk option or an open market — no middle option or dual market alternative was provided as a choice. Goodale was convinced by various studies that the Wheat Board

[9] *Colin Carter collaborated with Al Loyns on numerous grain market studies.*

would not survive if it had to compete with private traders in an open market. Justice Muldoon, in his Charter of Rights and Freedom ruling in 1996 also indicated, in his view, the CWB would not be viable in a dual market and the dual market would merely be a transition to an open market. The result of the vote showed 60% in favour of maintaining the Board. Finally the government and the CWB had a data set that supported their bias even though the survey question was the limited "either/or" option. That was enough for Goodale to stand his ground despite a rising tide of discontent.

The introduction of an open election for CWB directors was a new page in the on-going saga of the 70 year old organization. In typical WBGA fashion, when a door opens, they walk in. And that's what they did, by supporting a number of candidates in 1998 for election to the CWB District positions now being filled by a democratic vote. There were some close battles but Wheat Board supporters won out in all but one district. Nevertheless, the fortress wall had been breached. A WBGA sympathizer was inside the CWB stronghold. It was just one man, but he had an aristocratic ancestry ... and he was pissed!

If You Can't Beat 'em, Join 'em

Much of the success of the prairie farm groups was achieved when they were able to participate in the process. They formed organizations and sent representatives to various industry sessions to speak on their behalf. They joined larger groups and worked from inside the different organizations to drive change reflecting the wishes of their farmer members. They educated their members through newsletters and information sessions on commodity markets and the features and nuances of multiple programs and agencies that affected their bottom lines. They delivered the facts on transportation costs, grain standards, federal and provincial agencies, government policy, research and, yes, on the CWB.

In 1998, WBGA member and Penhold, Alta. farmer Jim Chatenay ran for the CWB Director position in District 2 on a platform supporting dual marketing. At the time he campaigned on his platform — "If you like the Wheat Board monopoly, don't vote for me!" He won, at least that's what the vote tally said. The Winnipeg welcome mat was not rolled out for Jim when he attended his first Board meeting at the CWB offices. But Jim was on a mission, a mission to get rid of one word from the lexicon of farming. That word? Monopoly!

Jim Chatenay's own personal issues with the CWB began over a skirmish with his permit book application. He filled it out, had it witnessed and sent it in only to have it rejected because the date on the application was a Sunday! Go figure.

"Are you kidding me?" he asked. But the CWB had no sense of humour. "It made me mad, and I found out I wasn't alone," Jim recalled. "I ran for the local Director position against a CWB "preferred candidate," but Alberta farmers didn't care about the CWB Directors' preferences. They just wanted the monopoly out of the way."

Jim expected a civil greeting from his fellow directors on that first meeting in Winnipeg, but quickly learned he was not at all welcome and his thoughts and suggestions proposing dual marketing or reduced regulations were wholly ignored. He was ostracized and frequently chastised by the chairman.

"I was pretty much on my own in Winnipeg; I had a lot of lunches by myself," says Chatenay. "There were several times I would come into a room of CWB Directors and they would send me out saying they were 'having a private meeting.' I was a Director, why wasn't I included? I got along really good with the staff, but I didn't see eye to eye with the elected people."

Chatenay recalls the looseness in which the Board operated. "When I got to Winnipeg, they didn't even have a budget. They just spent whatever they wanted to spend, and it was all farmer money." The disregard for the stewardship of farmers' money and failure to act in the best interests of all farmers really irked him. He felt alone as the sole true representative of farmers, and it was this responsibility that motivated him to keep working on their behalf. He served in the capacity for six years and was followed in District 2 by a fellow WBGA Director, Jeff Nielsen. The WBGA wasn't going to give up the seat at the table.

"What's astonishing to me," Chatenay says, "was it took 15 years, three elections and a whole bunch of people, barley growers, wheat growers, UGG and Cargill to change that one word — "monopoly", to get that word out of the way. But we did it!"

"The Board wouldn't budge on their position against a dual market option. By being so stubborn they actually lost the whole thing," he concluded.

"One of my favourite memories was the first Board meeting after I got out of jail for hauling my own grain into the United States," adds Chatenay. (more on this later, much more). "I got out after 23 days of the 64 day sentence based on good behaviour. My friends laughed and question that to this day. I decided to keep my "jail beard" and go to Winnipeg two days after my release. I opened the door and said, 'Hi guys, I'm back.' It really drove home my commitment to the cause. The room was dead silent, I can tell you that."

One Wagon Load for You — One Wagon Load for Me

It took six long years as a CWB director before Jim Chatenay got some help in Winnipeg. Finally, in 2006, another "choice" advocate claimed victory as a champion for dual marketing. Henry Vos defeated Art Macklin, ending his 15 year tenure as a director in CWB's District 1. The desire for change was gradually taking hold in more regions across the prairies but Vos' journey to that position differed from Chatenay's experience.

Chatenay had campaigned on a platform clearly stating he opposed the single desk exclusivity of the CWB. He represented a more open market perspective. Vos on the other hand knew he had to appeal to both right and left leaning farmers in order to get elected. He needed to appeal to the moderate, business oriented farmers. Vos avoided ties with farmer associations like the WCWGA and the WBGA to prevent getting labeled. His platform represented a more neutral stance, not just advocating for the end of the monopoly. His strategy was to get elected first and then move forward inside the CWB's Board with a solid, logical approach that would fairly represent the farmers in his area. Vos's vision was clear "Until you're on the inside you couldn't effect much change," he declared.

CWB's District 1 was a massive geographical region covering northern Alberta from the Yellowhead Highway to High Level in the north and west into the Peace River Region of British Columbia. The region did not have a cattle feeding industry or any domestic processing. Barley was a crop that grew very well there but the only buyer was the CWB, so marketing options were limited. The farm community was diverse and varied in their thinking but Henry knew if he stuck to fair and sound policy statements, he would gain enough support to win — and he did.

During the campaign Vos faced challenges from both sides of the philosophical debate. CWB friendly advocates demanded he declare his position on the single desk (which he deflected) while his colleagues on the right, who didn't understand his strategy, felt he was softening his stance in order to get elected. But Vos's vision was clear "Foremost in my mind was to get elected and then address the problems of the current CWB. I viewed my role as a director as providing a duty of loyalty and a duty of care in representing the farmers in my region."

In response to the challenges from old time farmers and directors of the CWB who demanded he support the CWB single desk mandate, he replied he understood the CWB's mandate but it was in serious need of some changes. He believed in the farmers' freedom to deliver grain whenever they wanted — with no quotas, no permit books, no restrictions. He believed market price would be the signal farmers should use to make their decisions.

It only required a bit of knowledge of Vos's ancestry to understand how deeply rooted he was in the concepts of market freedom and choice. Vos's maternal grandfather immigrated from England, settling in Lethbridge in the early 1900's. He was enamoured with the liberating concept of free range cattle feeding. When the government started dividing land into quarter sections and farmers started putting up fences, he moved north to Ferintosh. Within a few years the same thing happened there, so he moved to Keg River seeking open spaces and a less restricted lifestyle. For him, freedom to do what he wanted to do was most important.

Vos's father, Johnny Vos, was also an advocate of market freedom. He had been a teenager in Holland during the Nazi German occupation from 1939 to 1945. He was told what and when to do everything. The memory of that oppression stayed with him as he moved to Canada for a fresh start after the war. As a farmer he felt the CWB was a serious imposition in his life and represented an all too familiar level of control, one of a dictatorship he so strongly opposed. During the CWB's campaign to move canola under control of the CWB Johnny Vos spoke out against this move in favour of market freedom.

These are the ancestral roots that formed the views and position of Henry Vos as he followed

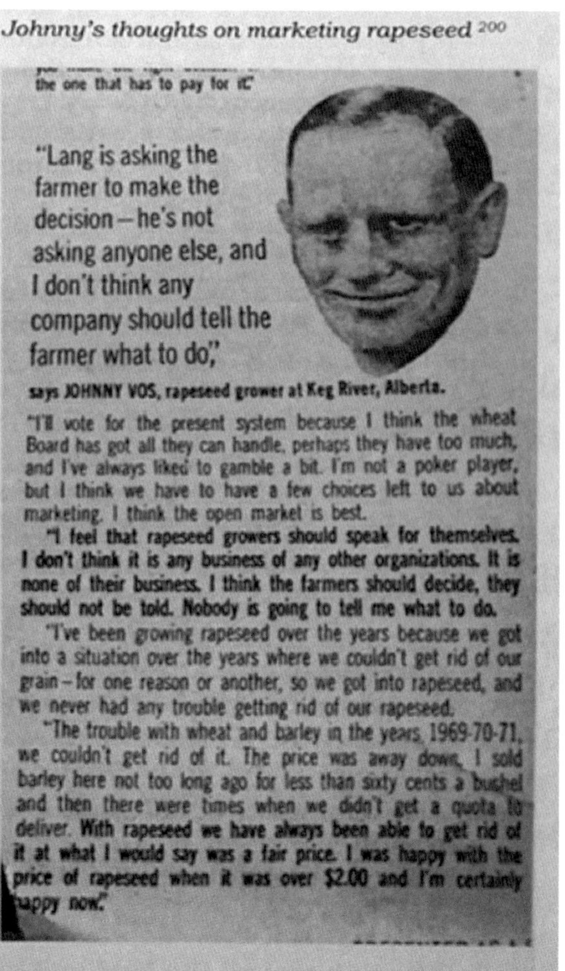

Johnny's thoughts on marketing rapeseed[200]

the one that has to pay for it."

"Lang is asking the farmer to make the decision—he's not asking anyone else, and I don't think any company should tell the farmer what to do,"

says JOHNNY VOS, rapeseed grower at Keg River, Alberta.

"I'll vote for the present system because I think the wheat Board has got all they can handle, perhaps they have too much, and I've always liked to gamble a bit. I'm not a poker player, but I think we have to have a few choices left to us about marketing. I think the open market is best.

"I feel that rapeseed growers should speak for themselves. I don't think it is any business of any other organizations. It is none of their business. I think the farmers should decide, they should not be told. Nobody is going to tell me what to do.

"I've been growing rapeseed over the years because we got into a situation over the years where we couldn't get rid of our grain—for one reason or another, so we got into rapeseed, and we never had any trouble getting rid of our rapeseed.

"The trouble with wheat and barley in the years 1969-70-71, we couldn't get rid of it. The price was away down, I sold barley here not too long ago for less than sixty cents a bushel and then there were times when we didn't get a quota to deliver. **With rapeseed we have always been able to get rid of it at what I would say was a fair price. I was happy with the price of rapeseed when it was over $2.00 and I'm certainly happy now."**

in their footsteps. Their independent views and the actions they took were the source of Vos's core values as he plunged himself into the belly of the beast as a director of the CWB.

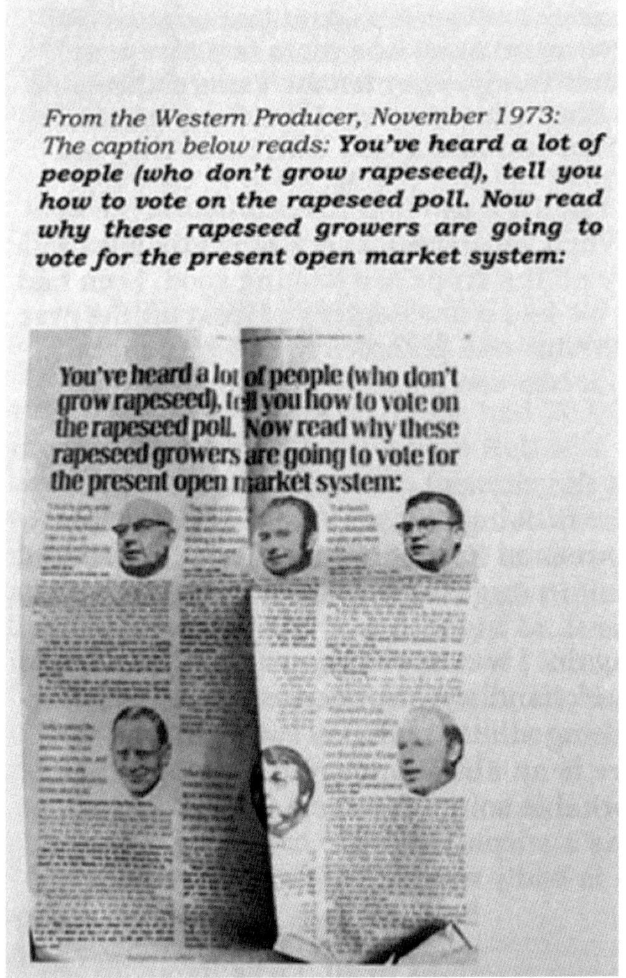

From the Western Producer, November 1973: The caption below reads: ***You've heard a lot of people (who don't grow rapeseed), tell you how to vote on the rapeseed poll. Now read why these rapeseed growers are going to vote for the present open market system:***

You've heard a lot of people (who don't grow rapeseed), tell you how to vote on the rapeseed poll. Now read why these rapeseed growers are going to vote for the present open market system:

Once inside the inner sanctum of the board of the CWB Vos encountered the same alienation Jim Chatenay experienced upon his arrival. Vos was considered an enemy of the CWB even though he was a Western Canadian farmer and a duly elected director. "Jim Chatenay was a great resource for me in the early weeks and months," recalls Vos. "He provided background on many topics and often told me what was said and what was really meant by the board's actions. They answered to no one, not even the farmers who elected them. They spent farmers' money however they wanted."

Things didn't change at all when, in 2008, Jeff Nielsen replaced Jim Chatenay as the District 2 director. The numbers at the CWB board table were still the same when it came to voting. "On business matters we tended to agree and generally made good decisions. But with two directors leaning to the right, five independents and eight left leaning ones the outcome on all political matters was a foregone conclusion. The "Crazy 8" voted as a block and maintained control," said Vos.

"That didn't mean we didn't have rousing discussions," recalled Vos. "I was often challenged with statements like 'If you're not for the single desk CWB mandate then you are against us.' Which wasn't true. I felt if the CWB continued down the road it was on, it wouldn't be around very much longer. Farmers needed choice and independence, not a guarantee of the same price as his neighbour."

"I challenged them on what "equal" meant. Was that one wagon load for me and one wagon load for you like they did when the CWB was first established? Then that means I can't deliver a second load until everyone has delivered their first load. Is that what you want? Well.... No, they would say, but it has to be equitable. Well what does that mean, I would ask. The debate went round in circles but the end result didn't change. The status quo remained."

The shenanigans continued with the eight hardline members of the board when the position of chairman changed. When Larry Hill retired as chair, Allen Oberg stepped forward to fill the vacancy. The announcement declared Oberg had won "unopposed". In a subsequent election Vos decided to run for chair, never expecting to win, but just to make sure they didn't describe the latest election as another unopposed win.

On another occasion the eight single desk supporters, feeling the heat of pressure to change, offered an olive branch deal with Chatenay and Vos. They proposed giving up CWB control of barley in exchange for an agreement whereby they and the federal government would drop the topic of removal of the monopoly on wheat for five years. "While I was considering the offer, Chatenay bellowed out 'No! Not a chance! It's all or none!' He sensed their weakening position and wouldn't deal."

"As the debate continued to escalate, the single desk directors started spending money on advertising campaigns. They directed money towards a bogus claim that the end of the CWB somehow threated the supply management sector in Eastern Canada and they came up with this crazy plan to hire a steam roller and send it to the parliament buildings in Ottawa suggesting the government was doing that to farmers in Western Canada. They were going to hand out flyers in Toronto and Montreal. At that point I stood my ground and said, 'absolutely not, that's not how we are going to spend farmers' money'!

Shortly thereafter, in the 2011 federal election, the Conservative party won a majority and both Henry Vos and Jeff Nielsen resigned from the board of the CWB. The hostility level in CWB board meetings had escalated as the single desk supporters got backed into a corner and became, in Vos's words, "ideological bullies". "I wouldn't be a part of that," Vos stated. "The debates became quite hostile and statements being made did not reflect my views and beliefs. Jeff and I had no choice. We had to resign. But we did so knowing change was coming and the end of the monopoly was finally in sight."

"I also had to resign in order to speak freely about my position on the matter, something I couldn't do as long as I was still a director," says Vos. "I also wanted to increase the momentum for this change to happen. My email inbox and phone were loaded with supportive comments after I resigned, confirming my beliefs and acknowledging the choices Jim and Jeff and I had made."

"Not all encounters between the WBGA and the CWB were bad ones," recalls Brian Otto, former WBGA President. "We had some great fun with Ian White at one of our annual conventions." White was hired by Minister Gerry Ritz as President and CEO of the CWB as part of their restructuring. He came from Australia, but he was no stranger to the Canadian grain industry. White had worked in Canada previously for Elders Grain and Saskatchewan Wheat Pool between 1987 and 1991. In Australia he developed his leadership skills acting as CEO of Queensland Sugar Ltd. in Brisbane. White made himself available to speak with anyone inside or outside the CWB. He focused on his job but retained an open mind to the bigger picture of agriculture. He was a breath of fresh air in a stagnate situation.

During White's tenure as the CWB's senior official, he was challenged with walking the tightrope of government policy to end the CWB monopoly, while at the same time providing the best governance for the organization. He understood the divisive circumstances of the monopoly debate and approached the job and its myriad of challenges with poise and balance.

"Ian was always available to speak with us," said Brian Otto. "Prior to his arrival, the CWB management let their ideology get in the way of making good business decisions. Ian reined that in to a certain extent with his "open door" policy. He was a great communicator and a reasonable person."

In 2011, without any discussion with farmers across the prairies, CWB management decided to spend $65 million of farmers' money to purchase two lakers to carry cargo on the Great Lakes-St Lawrence Seaway. This broadened the scope of business operations but was similar in some ways to their purchase of 2000 hopper cars in 1978-79 to facilitate an upgrade in railcar capacity. Although the need for hopper cars was critical, the driver to buy lakers was one of economic opportunity. Later that year, the laker acquisition was approved by White.

Source: AGCanada

"We had some fun with him in Calgary at the 2012 convention," Brian recalled. "Jeff Nielsen came up with the idea to present Ian with a sailor's hat to commemorate the CWB's new role as navigators of the sea! The WBGA Board presented him with this hat and then we all put one on ourselves. The whole room had a great laugh, including Ian."

The CWB barley trader, Bob Cuthbert, was in the audience and remembers the presentation. His reaction was a bit different. "I thought it was kind of silly, but at least they should have given him a captain's hat! Show some respect," he recalled buying into the prank.

By then, it was common knowledge the end of the monopoly would come about effective July 31, 2012 and August 1, 2012 would become Market Freedom Day. The mood in the convention room was jovial, even triumphant it could be said. Ian White's job still existed, as he was now in charge of "navigating" a new CWB, lakers and all. They didn't own any country elevators though and that would be a problem. But the barley farmers didn't really care about that. If the CWB could reinvent themselves and become a viable marketing alternative that would be excellent. They could provide a competitive alternative to the private grain companies. If they couldn't survive, as many CWB executives had predicted, that would only serve as proof the CWB didn't have the market power they professed. Either way, farmers stood to be in a better position after the monopoly was gone than the structure they were currently obliged to use.

A Dual Market or Market Choice

The concept of an open market wasn't new or unfamiliar to farmers in Western Canada. They existed all around them. From the public commodity exchanges and currency markets to prices for fertilizer and other crop inputs, the effects of supply and demand on price were a normal part of their individual risk management strategies. So when the WBGA lobbied for an open market or dual market or simply for market choice, they knew what they were asking for and how it would affect their businesses. They understood the potential gains along with the concomitant risks.

The real rub for the CWB came when they were forced to release public information on their activities. It didn't take long for analysts to discover things didn't add up. The quantity and quality of information coming out of the CWB after their restructuring in 1998 allowed for closer scrutiny of the organization's activities. Finally, factual data on sales, operational costs, activities and overall transparency was generally available. This new data added fuel to the fire for change.

CWB management tried to hide their mistakes or categorize expenses in creative ways, but the truths came out. Much credit goes to the CWB Monitor, a periodic analysis provided by market expert John De Pape who understood grain trading as well as, and likely better than, the CWB traders. His in depth analysis and tough questions really opened the door to questions of performance and accountability. And we've already talked about what happens at the WBGA when a door opens — that's right, they walk in.

From the very beginning, the WBGA advocated for market choice as opposed to the full removal of the CWB. They tried to work with the CWB to create win/win solutions. Their public position and press releases spoke to improving farmers' choices and they made sound arguments in describing the economic benefits of a dual market for Canadian feed and malt barley exports and domestic trade. While working with the Alberta Grain Commission in 2002/03 they prepared a strong economic case:

Economic Arguments

- The primary reason for pursuing marketing choice is economic. The CWB restricts marketing options for farmers, limiting their ability to manage business risks, and impedes value added investment.
- Marketing choice is not about getting the best price or a premium price or the top of the market. Marketing choice is about enabling individual decision-making and initiative in order to capture opportunities.
- Canada's economy is based on an open market environment.
- The pooling system of the CWB works on principle of wealth redistribution. As a result of this system, there is no incentive for farmers to be innovative in CWB grains. Price pooling also hinders producers who want to differentiate their product. A differentiated product can lead to self-generated premiums and less reliance on commodity markets.
- Multiple buyers for wheat and barley would create competition. Competition would result in greater efficiencies within the system, as well as increased returns for farmers.
- Farming is a business. Farmers need the ability to run their business without interference from the CWB.
- The viability of Canadian farms depends on farmers having flexibility. The need to be able to explore every possible opportunity appropriate for their own situation. Only individual farmers know what is best in terms of maximizing returns. The CWB cannot maximize returns for all farmers, as this would suggest picking the highest price of the year and selling all wheat/barley at this time.
- Canada is quickly losing market share. In order to compete globally, Canada must increase competitiveness.
- As farmers are facing ever-thinning margins, they need the ability to seek out new ways of doing business without the restrictions of the CWB.

These statements spoke to the nature of the problem, the outdated structure of the CWB and the need for change. Once again, the Alberta government was aligned with the WBGA in a collaborative manner but still some Western Canadian farmers lived in denial that changes were necessary or even prudent. They were unable or unwilling to acknowledge a problem existed.

Was There Ever a Problem with a Central Desk?

The essence of a disagreement boils down to two opposing viewpoints on a topic or position. Both opinions are based on their individual perspectives of the same issue but failing to agree on the outcome. Is one side or the other entirely, right? Is the truth somewhere in the middle? Or is there another agenda at play influencing beliefs? Other considerations worth noting include — What's at stake? What are the motives? Who stands to benefit?

In this particular case of dual marketing versus single-desk representation, the WBGA stood on one side of the debate and the CWB (their alleged agents) on the other. Western farmers on the whole were split on the matter. The farmers paid for the CWB to exist but aside from that had no say in the operations or performance of the agency. Was there a problem? Well there's that one for starters, but what about the actual performance of feed barley sales and returns to farmers? Was the CWB living up to its claims of capturing market premiums and leveraging its exclusive position for the benefit of farmers? Let's look at the numbers.

CWB Feed Barley Exports

The following chart is graphic evidence of the failure on the part of the CWB to expand or even maintain Canada's export feed barley market from 1970 through to the early 2000s. It was this concerning trend that triggered the WBGA's motivation for change in the mid 1970s. There are lots of excuses. The CWB have taken 'excuse making' to an art form since outsiders started challenging them. But prior to western farmers poking around, no one held CWB management and directors accountable for their actions — no one!

Statistics Canada's numbers don't lie. Canada's exports of feed barley hovered in a range of 2.5 to 4.5 million tonnes from the early 70's to the mid 80's. From the mid 80's until the early 2000's the picture became much more bleak.

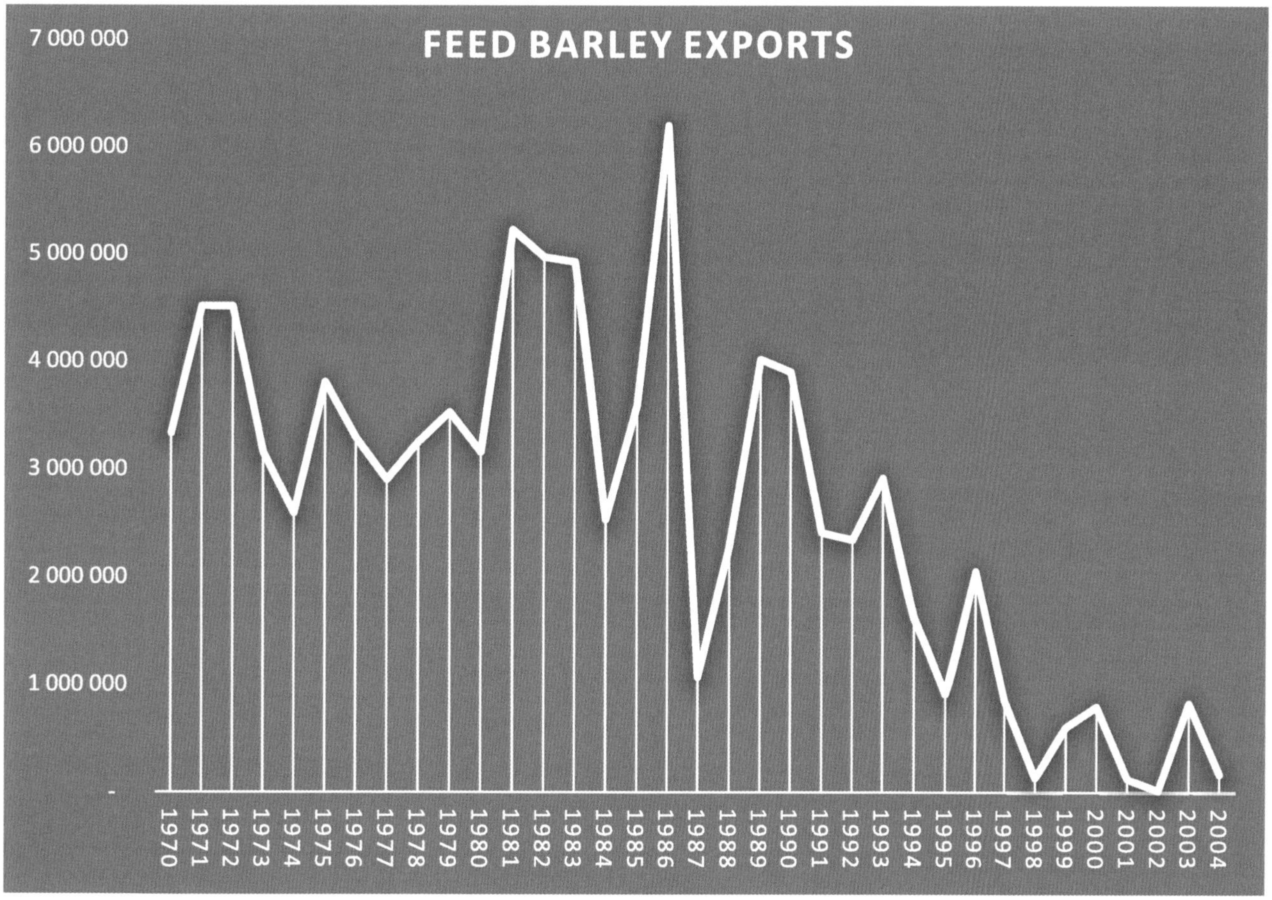

FEED BARLEY EXPORTS

7 000 000
6 000 000
5 000 000
4 000 000
3 000 000
2 000 000
1 000 000
-

1970 1971 1972 1973 1974 1975 1976 1977 1978 1979 1980 1981 1982 1983 1984 1985 1986 1987 1988 1989 1990 1991 1992 1993 1994 1995 1996 1997 1998 1999 2000 2001 2002 2003 2004

Source: Canadian Grain Commission — Canada Grain Exports 1970–2004

During this latter period, the CWB's operations continued to grow. At the same time, operating costs, borne by farmers, escalated, management salaries continued to be paid and inefficiencies and bad judgement reined supreme. Due to the precipitous decline in exports, returns to farmers maintained an extremely concerning downward trend.

From the annual reports of the CWB, available after the appointment of a new Board of Directors, farmers and the public were finally able to see real accounting results. Operational data, unavailable until the reports became public, showed numerous alarming trends and no apparent adjustment in expenses to address the declines in sales and financial success.

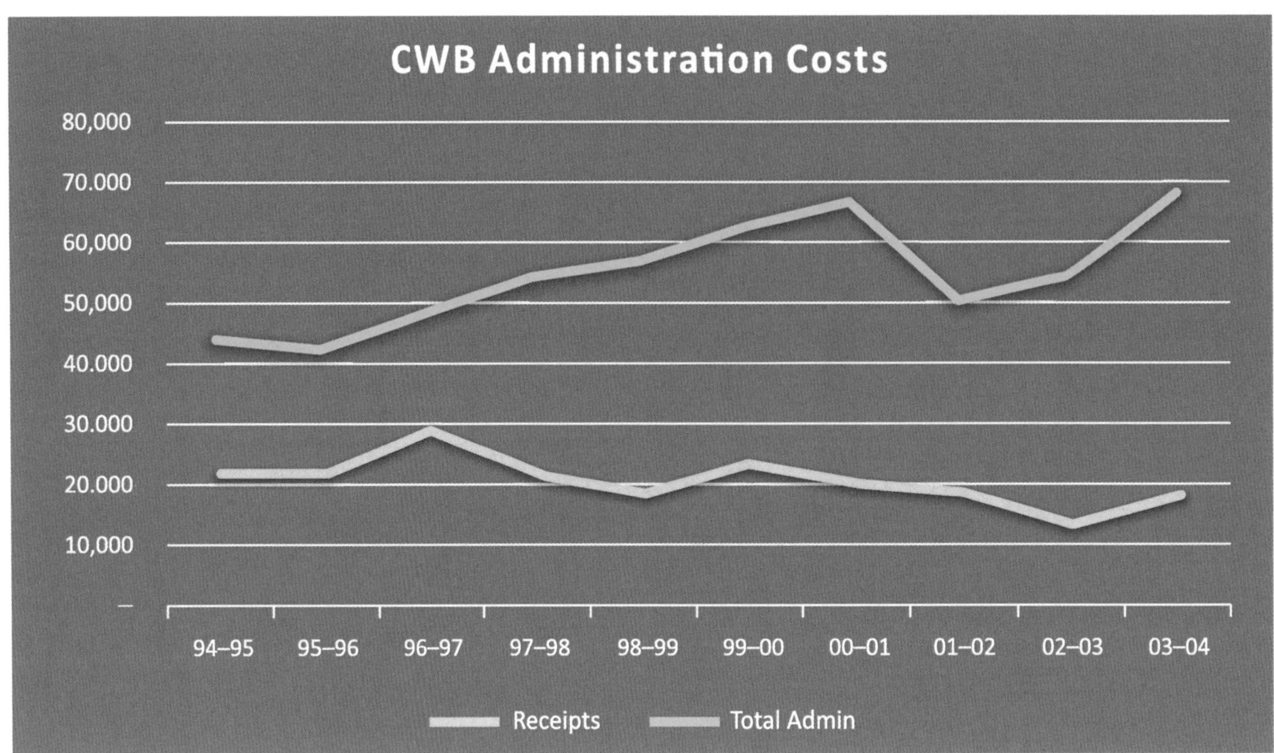

In the first ten years under the new CWB governance, grain receipts (wheat and barley) hovered around 20 million tonnes. CWB Administration costs escalated from $44 million dollars in the 1994-95 crop year ($2.00/tonne) to $67.6 million dollars in the 2003-04 crop year ($3.67/tonne).

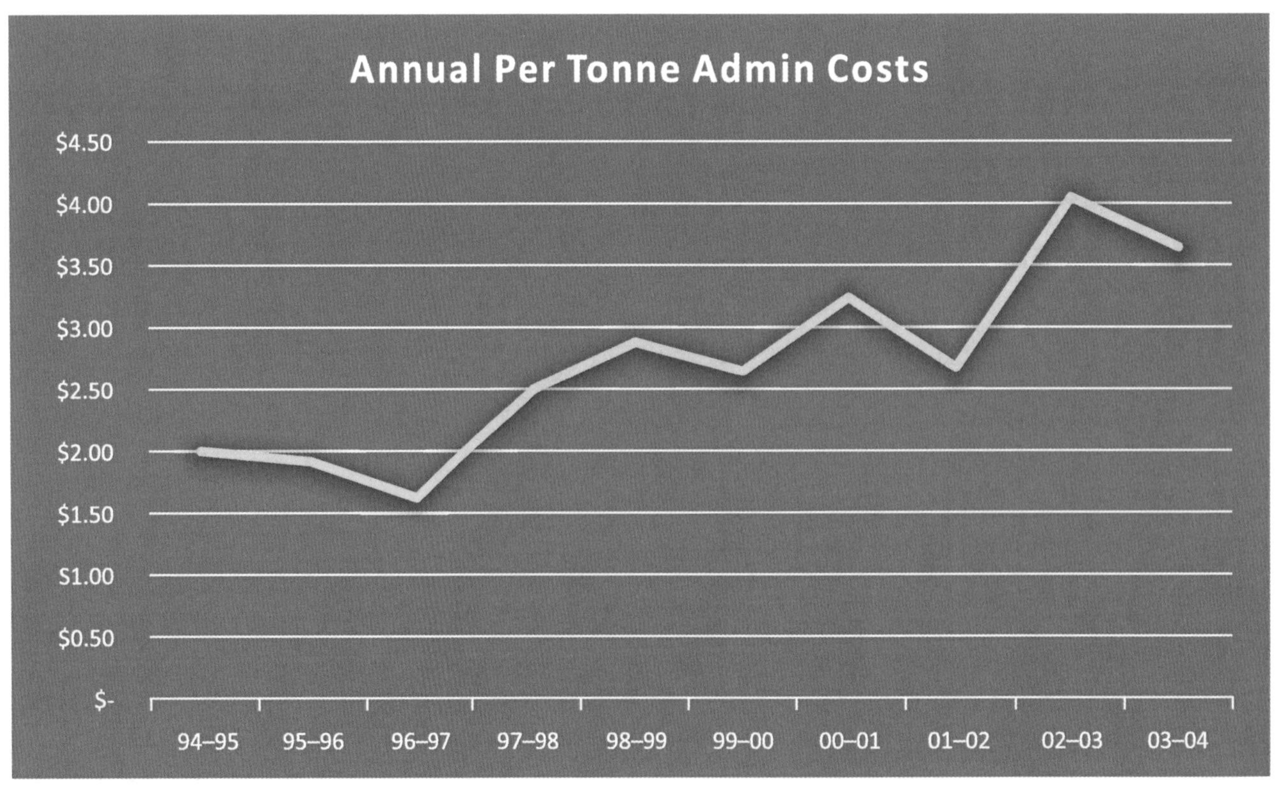

As the earlier chart shows in that same period, feed barley exports dropped from an average of 4 million tonnes to near zero. Based on this performance you wouldn't even hire the CWB to mow your lawn, never mind manage a multi million dollar export program.

It wasn't just that the WBGA felt like a dual market would be a nice option. The evidence was building and the trend was clear, the CWB was an epic failure when it came to marketing feed barley. A change was absolutely critical for its survival.

The contentious debate over the strategic value of a single-desk marketing agency versus an open or dual market waged on for years before the government action ended the monopoly. Its worth noting the opposition to change persisted, by those who supported the CWB, long after the Marketing Freedom for Grain Farmers Act was passed. But, as shown, numbers don't lie, and the following graph is strong evidence of a large and worsening problem. From a peak of exports in the 1985-86 crop year of 6.5 million tonnes, Canada's barley export performance deteriorated steadily. The drought in 2002 was a significant factor that year, but otherwise exports were disappointing, especially lower quality feed grade barley. The feed barley market was not being served.

The simultaneous growth of barley exports from Australia is evidence that a global market for feed and malt barley existed — and the Aussies were capturing the growth. The Australians modified their grading system to accommodate expanding Chinese demand while Canada held steadfast. Two opposite trends evolved and unfortunately, for Canadian farmers, they were on the declining side of the deals.

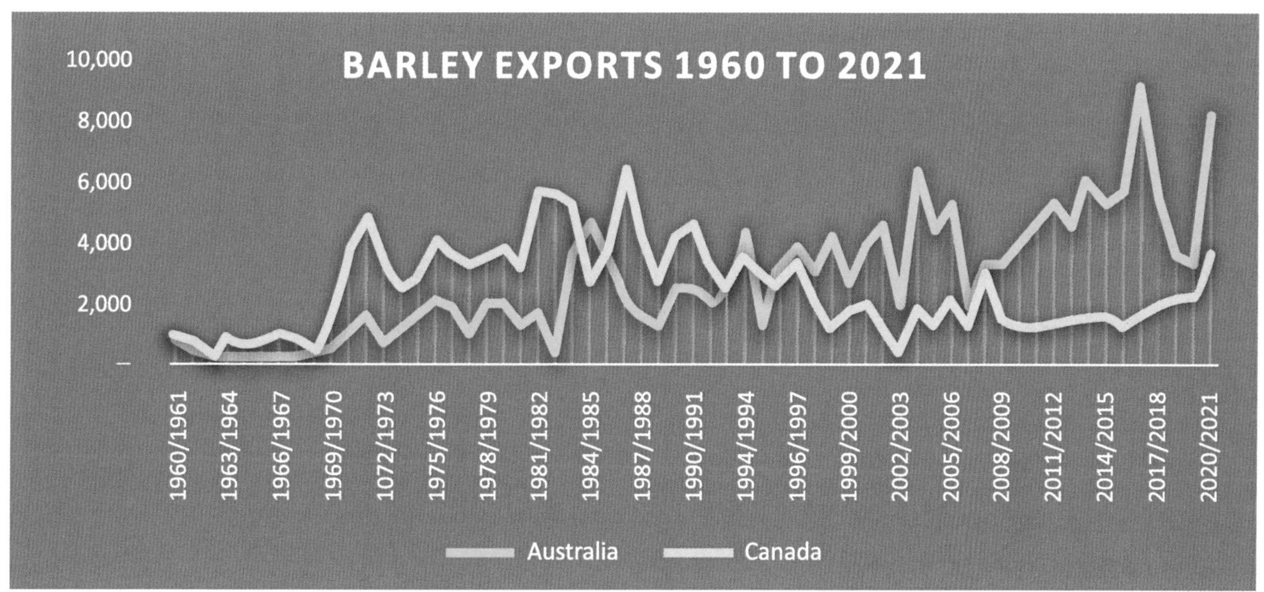

After the CWB monopoly ended, grain companies re-engaged in both feed and malt barley markets — especially the companies that owned export terminals who stood to gain another elevation at the export port. The feed barley industry had been ignored for many years, suffering from little to no market development or research for improved feed varieties to enhance yield or plant characteristics. Nevertheless, exports began to expand from 1.2 million tonnes in 2011–12 to 1.9 million in 2017-18, 3.0 million in 2018–19 and 4.6 million in 2020-21. The open market was working.

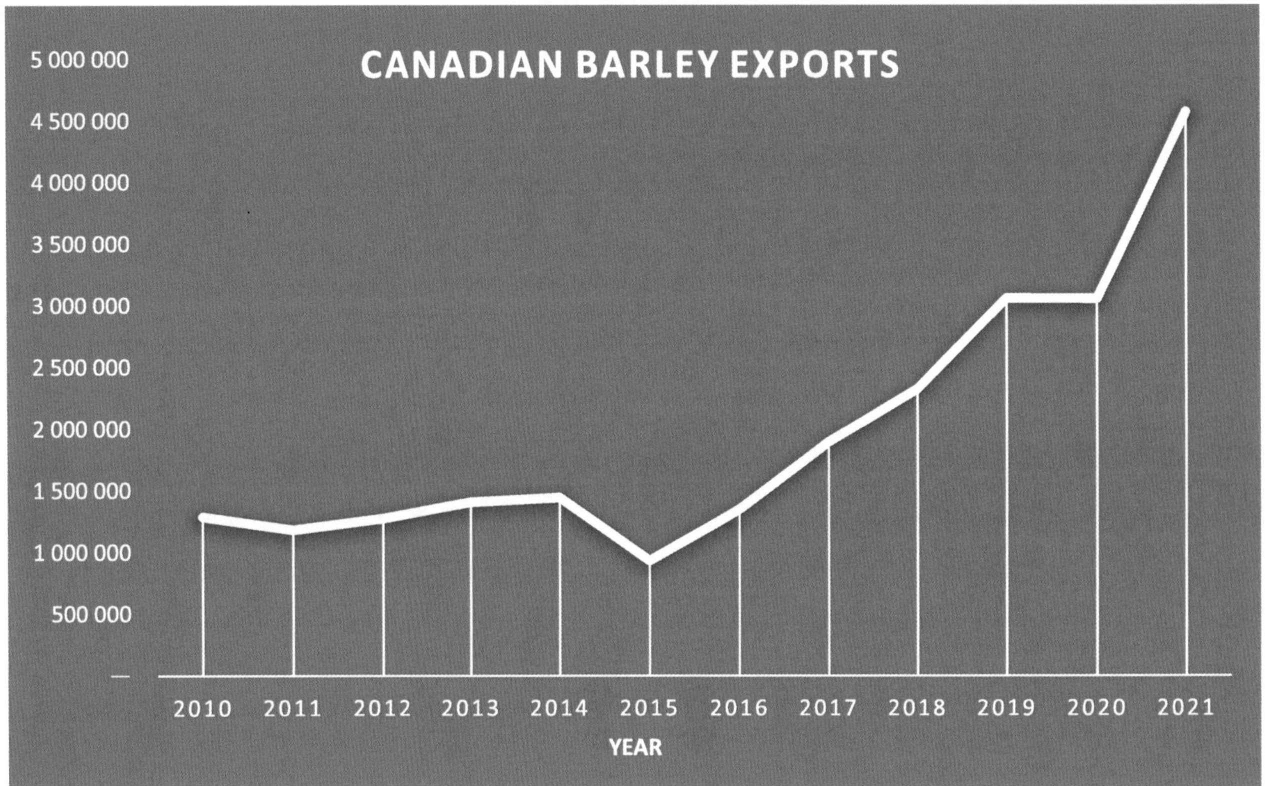

During the specific decade following the end of the monopoly, the newly named company, now referred to simply and legally as "CWB" began to falter. They attempted to make agreements with primary elevator companies to handle deliveries on their behalf on a fee for service basis, but they lacked control over the assets and were essentially competing directly with the service providers in their own driveways. This handling arrangement was doomed from the beginning.

The new CWB also purchased some country and terminal elevator capacity in an attempt to gain greater control over their marketing programs and supply chain. They purchased Mission Grain Terminal in Thunder Bay in 2013 and Prairie West Terminal in Dodsland in 2014, but the pickings were slim for small, independent elevators that could make a difference for the CWB. The larger grain handling companies were not the least bit interested in dealing assets to CWB enabling them to gain a foothold in country origination. In July 2015, the CWB announced a deal for a transfer of assets and control to a partnership of Bunge Corp and Saudi Agricultural and Livestock Investment Company (SALIC) Canada Ltd. This company was later renamed G3 and has grown significantly in both inland and terminal position since the acquisition.

In considering the ultimate demise of the CWB as it existed Jack Gorr recalled. "I never recommended getting rid of the Board[10] per se. But I was really surprised that it completely disappeared after the changes were made in 2012. Within five years the Canadian Wheat Board, as we knew it, was done."

The sale of the government owned agency to this new market entity in 2015 marked a closing chapter in the history of the Canadian Wheat Board. The market has taken a new direction in Canada, and most would agree it has been for the betterment of the Western Canadian farmers, and that was always the goal of the WBGA.

In answer to the question —"Was there ever a problem with a central desk?" —the answer is yes, most definitely. While export and domestic markets for canola and pulse crops thrived, the same could not be said for cereal grains, particularly barley. The unimaginative, lackadaisical approach of the CWB management was failing wheat and barley farmers and doing a disservice to Canada's economy. Farmers were feeling it and so was the entire value chain. From grain handlers to truckers to chemical companies to railways to export terminals, the problem had reached a critical juncture halfway through the first decade of 2000. From a single grassroots voice in 1977, the WBGA was now surrounded by contemporaries, by people and industry who shared their view that change was necessary, critical in fact. And one voice rose to the top as an industry watchdog over CWB activities, spotlighting the existence of problems and falsehoods better than any other during that period, using the CWB's own reports as evidence.

The CWB Monitor

The story of the final years of the CWB is not complete without a look back to one of the most compelling influencers of the changes ultimately introduced by the federal government. The CWB relied heavily on secrecy of their operations with limited public sharing of information related to their actions or their performance as an agent for the farmer. There simply wasn't enough factual data for a true accounting of CWB actions. But once the CWB was forced to release their annual

[10] *CWB*

reports, there finally was enough data for a seasoned trader and market analyst to start asking some tough questions about the CWB; enough data for John De Pape.

Mentioned earlier, De Pape began writing periodic articles in October 2010 that drew focused, critical attention to the actions and results of the CWB based on available facts and input from many of his trade contacts. This blog became known as The CWB Monitor. This passion project was ignited by De Pape's desire to provide clarity and a better understanding of the CWB issues ahead of the 2010 CWB director's elections. The WBGA and others immediately saw value in his work and urged him to keep digging and reporting.

"I felt pretty righteous about working with the WBGA; proud of the work we did together," admitted De Pape. "The one thing I remember was they knew they were right — and committed too. I remember one farmer telling me he didn't care if he made more money without the CWB. He just didn't want their foot on his throat anymore. Pretty graphic, isn't it."

Brian Otto was an ardent supporter of John's publication which was called the 'CWB Monitor'. "The WBGA really liked the messages, and the investigative work John was doing as he challenged the CWB in a weekly barrage," says Otto. At the time, De Pape had investigated the Board's performance of using the futures market in conjunction with its Fixed Price Contract (FPC) program. "Based on that work, the WBGA asked John to write a press release suggesting the CWB didn't have the knowledge or expertise to manage the Board's futures positions on public exchanges properly, particularly as they related to FPCs. The CWB immediately demanded a retraction. We asked John what he thought, and John replied emphatically, 'Don't retract anything. Ask them for a meeting.' So that's what we did."

The CWB senior management met with representatives from the WBGA along with John in their boardroom soon after, with Ian White chairing the meeting. "With John's support, we were able to prove quite convincingly that the CWB had really bungled their hedging program in Minneapolis wheat futures and the cost to farmers exceeded several million dollars," says Otto. "Ian got pretty quiet as the facts came to light. We never did have to provide a retraction."

With De Pape's help, the WBGA continued to "poke the bear" as Brian described it between 2010 and 2011. The CWB never spoke to John about his writings or asked him to retract anything after the initial meeting. They did try to track down who was paying him to produce his targeted entries, but their search was fruitless. That will remain a mystery, but in John's view, "It was just the right thing to do, and there was so much to write about!"

The Monitor covered a wide range of topics related to CWB actions (or inactions) including CWB expenses, the value of the single desk, the Contingency Fund irregularities, transactional mismanagement, the laker acquisition, the CWB plebiscite and the outlook for an open market.

The background was solid, and the questions, cutting. The defenders of the CWB were silenced time and time again by the factual, targeted arguments put forward by De Pape.

As an independent market analyst and commodity market specialist De Pape was in a unique position to challenge the Board. Unlike farmers or grain companies, he had nothing to lose by facing off with the Board and its senior management or marketing department. Over the two-year period John produced over 100 different blog posts addressing many areas of CWB responsibility and their failure to meet basic minimum levels of performance. He refuted their unsubstantiate claims with their own facts. Here is an example of one of those 100+ commentaries:

"#19 It's All About Listening and Responding (Oct 27, 2010)

Did you know?

For at least the last 12 years the CWB has surveyed farmers on a variety of issues, from attitudes about agriculture to preferred marketing systems.

The proportion of farmers who were surveyed over the years who support the status quo (single desk) on barley ranged from 22% to 36%.

The CWB has done nothing.

In January of 2007, CWB officials met with Minister Gerry Ritz in Ottawa. In attendance were senior officials from the malting companies and the President of the Malting Industry Association of Canada. These representatives explained that the malting industry would not invest any more capital in the malt industry in Canada as long as the CWB has single desk marketing authority. They were demanding changes.

The CWB did nothing.

The Canadian malt industry kept to its word and has not invested in any new capacity. However, since that time, China has built a great deal of capacity and continues to import Canadian malt barley and has now increased exports of malt dramatically. (From practically zero in 2004 to an estimated 375,000 tonnes in 2010.)

We have effectively exported our malting industry to China.

In March of 2007, the Federal Government held a non-binding plebiscite on barley marketing. Farmers voted and only 38% supported the status quo.

CWB Chairman Ken Ritter said:

"The results of the barley plebiscite announced today are not overly surprising. The CWB has been surveying farmers every year for the past 10 years and these results appear to be consistent with our annual findings."

The CWB has known farmers' views on the single desk for over ten years, and they have done nothing. They know the impact the single desk is having on the barley value added industry, and they've done nothing.

Earlier this year, the CWB hired a consultant to study the malt barley industry. The consultant apparently told the CWB:

The Pool and CashPlus need to offer producers better price signals.

The Pool and CashPlus need to offer malt companies improved delivery liquidity.

As far as I know, the CWB has done nothing with this study.

The CWB operates on behalf and for the benefit of farmers. Democratically, the majority of farmers have told the CWB over and over they don't want the single desk on barley; and the malt industry has told it in different ways what needs to be done to improve the malt industry (which also would benefit farmers). However, rather than act on any of this, the CWB does nothing but continue to argue adamantly that one of the options presented, the dual market, will not work. (I believe it can.)

This is all about listening and responding. Farmers know what is best for themselves. They need directors sitting at the CWB board table who won't override farmers' interests with their own ideology."

But we're getting a little ahead of ourselves here in telling the story of the WBGA. So much happened in the four decades preceding Market Freedom Day. The organization has a rich history of trials and tribulations on the long road to its ultimate destination. We've already heard some of their stories, but there are so many more...

Part 2

WBGA Initiatives

The Road to Marketing Freedom

A prairie road is an apt metaphor for the WBGA journey. They're typically long, generally straight and topped with perilous, loose gravel — sometimes too much, but mostly not enough. When the climate is unfriendly (rain or snow), they're messy and even more dangerous. When the future is unclear (storms or night falls), success is impeded. And when surprises occur (like unexpected friends of the four-legged variety), immediate and severe reactions to your direction may be required. When you encounter someone coming from the opposite direction, large or small, it's generally wise to slow down and even move over a little bit. You never really know how fast they are coming at you. And of course, there are always side roads, alternate paths that distract from your true path but may be important on their own, if travelled. All these characteristics apply to the challenges encountered by the members of the WBGA in their quest for market freedom.

It's a certainty that no one in attendance at the small, informal gathering at the Carseland Community Hall in 1977 could have predicted with any accuracy how long it might take to achieve their vision of an open market for barley. Five years? 10 years? 20 years? No one would have guessed 35 years! None of them could have imagined the hurdles they, and many more who followed in their footsteps, would face or the sacrifices required to clear a path for marketing freedom. It was inconceivable to foresee the CWB, the very agency charged with representing the best interests of all farmers, would turn on them so aggressively and deny them those things considered normal business operations in the rest of Canada outside the Designated Area. No one expected their pleas to a democratically-elected federal government would fall on deaf ears. But that was exactly happened. This was the path taken on the WBGA's road to marketing freedom.

Taking on a new challenge is both exhilarating and scary. It's like riding a roller coaster for the first time or learning to drive. But there are things you can do to prepare yourself, things that will dampen the scary part while amping up the exhilaration. Surrounding yourself with positive, like-minded people is one of those supportive things. So are focusing on the things that matter and things you can control. If you dwell on all the reasons why you might fail, chances are you probably will.

The founding members of the WBGA focused on the positive and sought out fellow farmers who had similar views and were known to be dedicated hard workers. Good fortune and a clear vision were also important in their mission. That doesn't mean to say there weren't roadblocks and potholes along they way. In fact, there were many. But these folks had perseverance in spades and collaborated to achieve their goals.

WBGA members jumped on the roller coaster with arms in the air and the wind in their faces. They intended on hanging in there until the ride was over. And they were joined by many others along the way.

Dual Marketing

Let's start by being clear on the goal. As stated, the mission of the Western Barley Growers Association was not to abolish the Canadian Wheat Board. According to Past President Brian Otto (and echoed by numerous other WBGA members), "The sole vision of the original builders of the WBGA was market freedom. Farmers needed more freedom to choose when, where, how and to whom they sold their grain. The very thought that they didn't really own the grain they produced was repugnant to the independent minds of the pioneers and innovators who farmed land in Western Canada."

Ironically, the primary barrier to fulfilling this vision was the Canadian Wheat Board Act. The CWB, as the operating agent, enjoyed the support of the politically left-leaning parties who have largely dominated the electoral landscape in Canada since the CWB was established. Apart from periodic Conservative governments, the legislation of Canada has been Liberal either in power or as the opposition to a minority government.

After the Second World War, the CWB shifted its focus from assuring wheat supplies to allies during the conflict, to acting as the marketing agent for farmers in the Designated Area of Western Canada. From the very beginning, CWB Directors and their senior managers were clear in their opposition to the concept of dual marketing. They stood fast in their view that an open market and single desk selling could not co-exist. By definition, the single desk is the antithesis of an open market. People inside and outside the CWB shared a view the agency itself could not exist in an open market. Without the single desk monopoly powers, the CWB would be impotent, unable to provide any value. To that end, the CWB fought vigorously to defeat any attempt to reduce their power and exclusivity. The farmer led prairie pools[11] shared this view and sided with the CWB, while the other grain companies remained mostly neutral.

The exception in the co-operative grain handler ranks was United Grain Growers who leaned more towards an open market, favoured by many of their farmer members. In their view, the business reality was obvious. All grain companies were beholden to the CWB for large tariff handling and storage revenues as well as terminal earnings on CWB exports. Any move away from this structure to one of diminished power for the CWB could result in reduced revenues for the status quo grain handlers. They would have to compete in a more open market which was welcome by some grain companies while simultaneously feared by others.

The prairie pools operated as warehousemen, not commodity traders. They left that task to the CWB and focused their operations on blending gains and larger volumes inland and again at the ports. Senior managers knew they lacked the expertise to develop their own grain marketing departments and compete in the international marketplace. It was a clear choice for most of those organizations to align with the CWB.

[11] *Manitoba Pool, Saskatchewan Wheat Pool and Alberta Wheat Pool.*

A sidenote is in order here to pay tribute to Ted Allen in his role as president of United Grain Growers. UGG was a prairie pool, but any comparison to the provincial co-ops ended there. UGG initiated new, innovative programs and listened to the needs of their members. Allen spoke on behalf of farmer members of that organization even if that was against the policies and programs of the Canadian Wheat Board. He offered insight on the positions taken by the CWB and the Canadian Federation of Agriculture on the international stage and was instrumental in developing the Canadian Agri-Food Trade Alliance in 1997. "CAFTA" became a voice for farm commodity groups who were not aligned with Canada's powerful supply management groups on the international stage. This later proved very helpful in dealings with the World Trade Organization nearly a decade later.

Ted Allen

Doug Robertson recalls another incident where Allen clashed with the CWB. "UGG was the first to install protein testers for wheat in their elevators so farmers could get a fairer quality-driven price. Not long after the three Pools bitched to the CWB that this method of attracting grain to their opposition's elevators was "unfair", I remember coming into the Olds UGG one day as they were removing the protein tester. When I asked what they were doing I was told "You farmers just paid for one of these in every elevator in Western Canada thanks to the Pools — the CWB just bought us all one with your money!". I think the price was around $60,000 apiece, but not positive on the price. In any case, usually what the Pools wanted, they got, and Ted Allen and UGG undoubtably paid for their pro free market farmer attitudes with punishment by the CWB many times."

The CWB developed a special delivery levy collection of $.50/tonne on deliveries of 1 CW Red Spring and 1 CW Amber Durum collected at export position as a "protein equipment pool". They also provided the industry with an estimated cost of $3 to $4 million of farmer money would go towards the cost of the equipment. This estimate fell well short of the grain company estimate of $30 million to bring the system up to standard.

In the early years of the barley growers' organization, the seemingly radical views of the WBGA resulted in difficulty securing allies in the industry. But once the WBGA's messaging became more widely distributed, companies took a side, either actively supporting or opposing their proposals. This serendipitously included several nascent, innovative grain dealers, like-minded groups such as the Palliser Wheat Growers[12] and even some aligned corporate entities like the Winnipeg Commodity Exchange.

In building the case for their proposed changes to the CWB monopoly, the WBGA clearly stated the barley market is very different from the wheat market. Very little barley is used as human food; most of it is fed to livestock. Unlike wheat, which is mostly exported, the primary and most stable market for barley is "on-farm use" and the domestic feed market, which usually takes more than half of the annual production. The CWB was doing a sub standard job in selling export feed barley. There was really no downside in promoting a more open market in the eyes of barley producers. Could it get much worse? Actually, yes. As the years wore on it did get worse as exports continued to decline and returns to farmers decreased. But still the old guard at the CWB held on in defense of a misguided marketing system that was failing the farmer.

The proposed introduction of a dual market had many features and benefits for barley farmers, including a broadening of grain marketing choices, a strengthening of both export and domestic channels through the dissemination of better information and market signals and, perhaps most critical to many, improved cash flow options. As much as the CWB tried to shoehorn the "one model fits all" approach to grain marketing of barley, this strategy was failing miserably.

The WBGA acknowledged the CWB treated wheat and barley differently, but not in a positive way. While malt barley sales were prioritized just like wheat, the feed barley market was largely overlooked. That was the case year in and year out, excluding occasional years when building barley surpluses required some export sales for the express purpose of reducing inventories. The WBGA communicated their views to the CWB, to government and anyone else who would listen, but their pleas went unheard. The system suited those who preferred to offload their marketing tasks to the single-desk model but allowed no alternatives for others to explore. Advocates of the single desk believed there was market power in confining offers to one seller. In their view, the economics of supply and demand meant little in comparison to their perceived view of the one seller/multiple buyers view of price determination.

From the early 1980s, the WBGA offered some rather detailed recommendations describing how a dual market might function, including necessary changes to the current pricing and delivery

[12] *Later renamed the Western Canadian Wheat Growers Association*

options offered by the CWB. For example, they recommended a delivery-specific contracting approach which would provide some aspect of choice and more certainty to farmers regarding price and delivery. This contractual approach could also be an improvement for CWB's own marketers who were never confident barley farmers would deliver grain into the quota system at all.

The debate over the pros and cons of dual marketing raged on for more than a decade, well into the 90s. Numerous studies and surveys commissioned by both the WBGA and, later in the early 1990s, the Alberta Barley Commission (ABC), convinced the Alberta Government and the Alberta Grain Commission to speak out on behalf of farmers. Marketing meetings were held across the province of Alberta and the clear trend among all of them showed a strong majority of farmers in Alberta wanted a voluntary grain marketing system.

In August of 1989, the WBGA was buoyed by the announcement of the removal of oats from the exclusivity of the CWB. The reasoning given was oats had become a relatively small, specialized crop, too small for the CWB to administrate. Removing barley seemed like an inevitability to the WBGA on the same grounds but CWB management and directors didn't see it that way.

In February 1990 the independent farm weekly, Agriweek, published an article suggesting the CWB needed to embrace dual marketing. This article was reprinted in the WBGA newsletter for their annual convention. In his editorial, Morris Dorosh challenges the CWB to back up their boasts of securing premiums for Canadian sales due to the single desk...

"It is the lot in life of everyone affected by the operation of the Board that there is no impartial means to determine whether the Board is being run well or poorly, except for such self-congratulatory oratory as issued from the wheat pool annual meeting a couple of weeks back.

It would be different if the Wheat Board were not a monopoly. If farmers had legal alternative methods to sell their grain and if grain buyers had legal alternative methods to buy it, it would soon be seen which system works best. But even the mere mention of any kind of dual, freedom-of-choice marketing tends to throw many of the Boards supporters into tantrums.

If the Board is so confident of its grain selling prowess, why would it fear dual marketing of, say, export barley? Why would it not welcome, indeed even eagerly seek, the chance to show how it can demolish competition in truly competitive, level-playing-field circumstances? Would it not rather settle this business once and for all, into the bargain also improving the odds that other crops[13] might soon be added to its mandate?"

[13] *There was discussion of moving canola under the exclusive, single-desk management of the CWB.*

The ultimate goal of the dual market proposal was a shift to market driven pricing. Supply and demand would become meaningful, and the effects visible. Transportation shortages or surpluses could also impact the net price to farmers and the domestic trade would reflect world values, providing competitive markets and accurate values. Planting decisions could be made with more certainty of value and shipping. The CWB would have to compete on a level playing field with private grain companies and the domestic markets. It seemed like a good idea to most barley growers, especially those closer to domestic feed and malt buyers, but it didn't resonate well with growers on the fringe of the Designated Area and most definitely not with the monopolistic management of the CWB.

It also seemed like an idea whose time had come to the new Manitoba-based federal Minister of Agriculture, Charlie Mayer, as he stepped into his new position in January 1993. He and the Conservative Party were more sympathetic to the requests of the WBGA and the Western Canadian Wheat Growers Association than the Liberals. But later that year Canada's political landscape changed dramatically and with it any hope for change within the ranks of the WBGA.

In that year, Liberals annihilated the Progressive Conservatives who not only lost their majority of 169 seats but only managed to win two seats in the election. That's right — two seats! Even the NDP only managed nine seats, their worst showing in history. Regional parties rose in popularity in the form of Bloc Quebecois and Reform and Jean Chrétien won a Liberal majority. This election also placed the Liberal MP for Regina-Wascana, Ralph Goodale as Minister of Agriculture. As a western-based minister, his appointment should have been well received by farmers, but his rigid view on protecting the CWB's monopoly was a crushing defeat for the WBGA's dual marketing movement. Safe to say, you won't find Ralph Goodale's name on the list of Friends of the WBGA.

Some Detours Along the Way

Unfortunately, roads can also be counted on for delays and detours, and so too was the WBGA's plan for dual marketing. The election of the Liberal majority in 1993 and the colossal failure of the short-lived Continental Barley Market[14] in August of that year were clear signals to the WBGA that their hopes and dreams of a dual market had suffered a setback — a serious one.

Fortunately, for the WBGA and Western Canadian farmers, they had a number of other important files in the works besides marketing freedom. The deeper they dug into factors affecting

[14] *The Continental Barley Market action was a federal government initiative to open trading for feed and malt barley between private grain companies and buyers in the United States. More on this topic to follow.*

the barley industry the more they realized there were a lot of farm-related issues besides dual marketing, a lot of areas in which farmers needed to take on a greater role in developing and even managing. So the WBGA put their dual marketing dreams on hold as they addressed other topics. Fortunately, the Alberta Barley Commission would be approved soon providing the barley sector with an important injection of farmer capital from the new levy. This funding would provide the Alberta barley sector with a war chest to press for change and equal rights with farmers across Canada.

Alberta Barley Commission (1991)

A constant challenge faced by small commodity-based associations is sustainability. Their financial viability is generally dependent on memberships, fund raising activities (like conventions) and sponsorships along with any government support they can muster. Fundamental to attaining positive cash flow in an association is the requirement to continue to be relevant. Contributions to an association are based on perceived value, and so, by that measure, and with 44 years of continuous operations, the Western Barley Growers Association is an undeniable success. But that success hadn't been without its challenges and they had yet to achieve their primary objective.

In the mid 1980s the concept of a provincial barley commission was raised at a WBGA Board meeting. Producer-funded commissions existed for other commodities, and it made sense to try to formalize a revenue stream from all barley farmers to augment other sources of funds. If the barley industry was going to expand and prosper, then the growers needed to take matters into their own hands to ensure that happened. Upon further internal discussion, the WBGA Board felt launching a provincial barley commission in Alberta would allow farmers to collect funds and target investments toward important programs including research, market development and education. Strategically they determined it was preferable to retain the politics of the barley industry within the WBGA, leaving the development work under the auspices of the new commission thus creating an important distinction between the two organizations with the commission being a less biased, non-political entity.

However, there was a problem. "The WBGA could have gotten a commission established relatively easily earlier on in the 1980s," says Doug Robertson. "But the only levy option at the time supported by the federal Farm Products Council of Canada (FPCC) was a mandatory checkoff like the Cattle Commission, and that went against WBGA philosophy to allow producers to 'vote with their feet' by asking for their checkoff back if they didn't like the direction the Alberta Barley Commission was going. Until a voluntary checkoff was allowed, the WBGA wasn't interested." And there were further hurdles the WBGA had to clear to achieve their vision of a producer driven barley commission.

"Once a refundable check-off was allowed, information reached WBGA that the feds were thinking of establishing a checkoff system on wheat and barley for the prairies," he continues. This would eventually become the Western Grain Research Foundation. "The WBGA feared any federal checkoff system would not be in the best interests of Alberta barley farmers since the federal ag scene was dominated by the Canadian Federation of Agriculture and the CWB."

In the past, barley was always the "weak sister" of grains and oilseeds — funding always went to wheat, oilseeds and special crops first — barley was "just food for cattle". The CWB would insist that no checkoff funds could go to anything but research, to keep others out of their territory in the areas of policy, marketing and beyond. A prairie-based levy system covering all crops was definitely not the preferred option of the WBGA.

It was no secret Alberta was never CWB-friendly territory, so it was also expected — at least by Albertans — that most of the research money allocated by the CWB would flow to Saskatchewan first, then Manitoba, then Alberta following the CWB's order of preference. The WBGA felt it was critical for funds to be made available for policy initiatives to fight things like the CWB monopoly, and to get some core funding for the WBGA so that they wouldn't have to depend solely on producer membership dollars to do policy work. The original concept was for the ABC to employ WBGA to do its policy work. That was the WBGA's plan, but it didn't turn out that way.

After two and one half years of planning and conducting FPCC-required province-wide producer meetings, led mostly by Stan Wiskel and other WBGA personnel, the newly formed Alberta Barley Commission (ABC) was launched on August 1, 1991. The organizational meetings were especially fractious in the northern part of the province where CWB support was the strongest. "Stan was exceptionally sharp and very committed to the development of the commission," recalls Alberta government analyst Charlie Pearson. "I remember times when I would see him in the audience whenever I was making presentations in the Boyle area. I knew I was in for some stingers from him," he laughs. "There was definitely a scud missile or two headed my way from Stan." But, like so many other WBGA volunteers of association initiatives, Stan became the heart and soul of the Alberta Barley Commission initiative.

Most of the meetings in those regions were stacked with a number of supporters brought in by the CWB to try and prevent a WBGA-sponsored commission from being established. Doug Robertson remembers one meeting where the CWB attempted to disrupt proceedings and the ABC called on the WBGA for their support. "The CWB bussed in over 40 people to an ABC Annual General Meeting to try and pass a motion preventing the Commission from getting involved in policy. The WBGA members rallied to support the ABC against the CWB's tactic despite our differing opinion on who should take the lead on policy. ABC was better than the CWB by a long way!"

Eventually, the rebellious nature of Alberta farmers and a convincing presentation by the WBGA team resulted in the farmer majority required to form a commission. Efforts to motivate groups in Saskatchewan and Manitoba to form their own barley commissions failed, so it was up to Alberta barley farmers to break trail on important work which would benefit all barley growers across Canada.

Despite the WBGA establishing ABC, in part as a way to access stable funding, their vision never materialized. The new ABC Manager and Executive ultimately opted for ABC to conduct its own policy work. Some money for conventions was allocated to the WBGA, but that was it. The benefits of having a commission became evident over the years, but a jurisdictional struggle developed between the WBGA and the ABC. All policy development that the WBGA had hoped would stay with them was taken up by the newly-formed commission.

The roles of the two organizations became confusing for barley growers who predictably assumed ABC was replacing the WBGA. Membership in the WBGA started to decline steadily once the ABC was established, as barley farmers felt they were paying for everything via the check-off. "I'm already giving you guys money in the checkoff. Why should I pay for a WBGA membership too?" was a frequent question from Alberta barley farmers at the time.

The first Chairman of the ABC and former President of the WBGA, Tim Harvie, recalls the early days of the Commission. "Some felt there was room for both barley organizations in Alberta but trying to maintain both entities became confusing for farmers. We had a responsibility to manage farmers' money carefully and that determined how we ran the commission," he says. In 1993 and beyond, the WBGA and ABC were able to work together during the Charter Challenge as they aligned in an attempt to prove the unconstitutionality of the CWB.

But despite this brief comradery, the rift between the two Alberta based barley entities continued in the ensuing years. Robertson elaborated "The ABC Executive pressed the WBGA to sign an agreement to disband WBGA if they could not prove they had at least 500 paying producers as members. After preliminary discussions, WBGA President Buck Spencer told them to go to a rather hot place," recalls Robertson. "Later, at the ABC's 1998 Annual General Meeting the Delegate System was passed, preventing anyone but ABC delegates from presenting resolutions from the floor. This reduced discussion and further shut out WBGA members and its board from ABC procedures."

Future WBGA directors attempted to resolve the divide between the two organizations but they were unsuccessful. Mike Leslie[15] took over as the ABC General Manager in 2005 and worked towards reconciliation between the two organizations but he quickly recognized the challenges the position carried with it. "I discovered most of the requests for levy refunds were due to the feeling the ABC was too anti CWB," Leslie said. "I knew the ABC had to remain as politically neutral as possible in order to represent all barley growers respectfully. The ABC sponsored some WBGA activities over the years I was at ABC, but there was a clear distinction in mandates between the two entities."

The ABC continued to provide important value for Alberta barley farmers over the years with different management and directors accomplishing valuable and important work for barley farmers, but the issue of marketing freedom was not addressed. The original purpose of the WBGA's formation, over twenty years ago, was still unresolved. The specific goal of the WBGA's founders remained unfulfilled and the Alberta Barley Commission was not going to be the solution. There was still work to be done.

The Saga of Feed Barley to the USA (1992-1996)

In 1992, southern Alberta farmer Buck Spencer knew the price for domestic sales of barley to feedlots and feed mills in the province of Alberta. And he also knew the price of barley in northern Montana and Idaho and it was much higher there. A significant difference in local feed barley values existed, delineated by the forty-ninth parallel, nearly $30/tonne in fact, or 37.5% higher in Canadian dollars. Spencer also knew the reason for the difference — the Canadian Wheat Board's low price and their inability to provide markets for the barley Alberta farmers had grown. The CWB's inaction created a ceiling on barley prices with no option to capture a market opportunity just a few miles away, across the Canada/U.S. border.

[15] *Mike Leslie passed away after being interviewed for this book but prior to its publication*

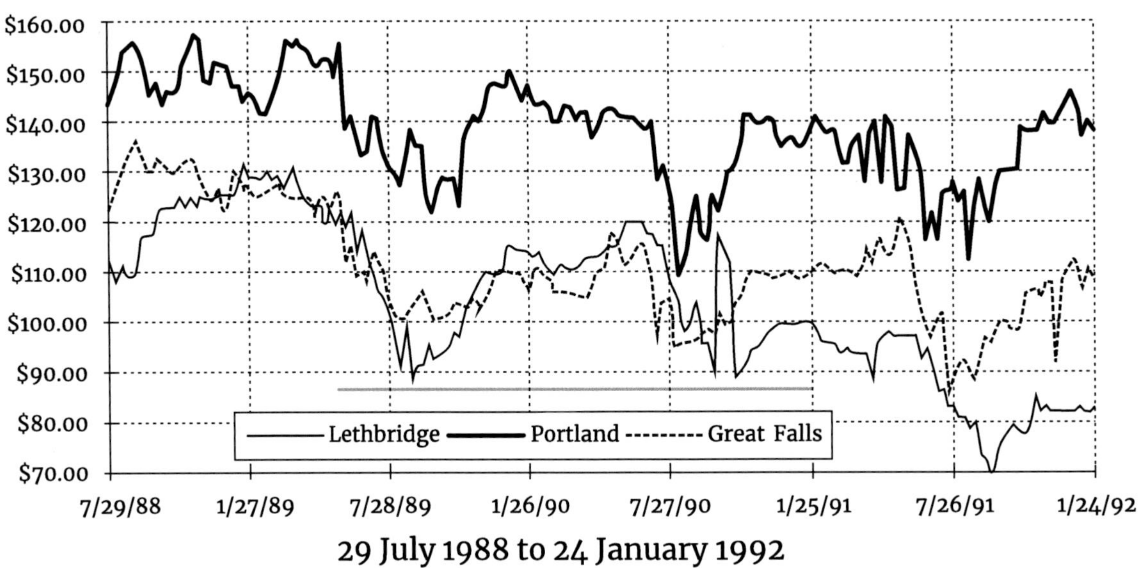

Spencer's extensive knowledge stemmed from the fact that he'd been shipping barley to the U.S. for several years, all completely legally of course. He contracted with the CWB to buy back his barley from them at their export price and he incurred the freight cost to his U.S. buyer's destination, along with customs and brokerage fees at the border. He incurred fuel costs to deliver his barley and even purchased a Montana diesel permit. He did it "by the book", in line with CWB requirements, border customs regulations as well as export laws.

Buck Spencer lost money on every load when he added everything up. He lost $892.50 in 1989, $165.91 in 1991 and $113.06 again later that year. But that wasn't the point. If he wasn't required to pay the CWB export price to buy back his own grain he would have profited on each load. "But that's not how the pooling system works," you say? That's true, but Spencer's intention wasn't to prove he could make more money shipping to Shelby, Montana. It was to demonstrate markets existed for Canadian barley and the CWB wasn't doing its job. These were potentially large, profitable markets.

Spencer's history in the U.S. barley market went back a couple of years. In 1991, a trucker and rancher from Jerome, Idaho named Herb Allen contacted Spencer with an interest in buying one million bushels of barley. He indicated additional, ongoing demand in the years to come. Plus, Allen was only one of several U.S.-based clients interested in buying Canadian barley. This discovery was of particular interest to the directors of the WBGA as well as the agriculture ministry of the Alberta government because it offered the opportunity to export more grain produced in Alberta and put more money in the pockets of Western Canadian farmers.

The Alberta government developed policies to push back on the federal clutches on agriculture within their province. Once every year, representatives from Alberta's Agriculture Ministry would send a small contingent of staff and elected officials to Winnipeg to meet with the CWB. In January 1992 that contingent was slightly larger than normal; in addition to seven Alberta Agriculture staff and the Minister of Agriculture for Alberta, Ernie Isley, they were joined by four WBGA directors and Herb Allen, the Idaho feeder. Their goal was to meet with the CWB to discuss ways and means to seal this deal and capture a new opportunity. How could the CWB object?

"Isley[16] got right into it with the CWB commissioners," recalls Buck Spencer. "He said 'You've always said you want to help us. Well, we've got Buck Spencer here who produces barley and Herb Allen here who wants to buy it. Let's make a deal!" Cutting through all the back and forth and sleight of hand from the CWB, ultimately, they had no interest in negotiating concessions to facilitate this new market or allow farmers to export their own grain outside the current "buyback" system. They defended their decision on the basis of the CWB Act. In Buck's words, they "hid behind the Act."

The harsh reality was government regulations continued to defeat individual farmers who desired the dual market option as it was proposed by the WBGA. The single-desk structure of the CWB and their export buyback philosophy continued to stand in the way of individual farmer's freedom of choice and personal marketing needs for wheat and barley. The "best for all those involved" philosophy prevailed even though it was unproven. Speaking on behalf of the CWB, Commissioner Richard Klassen, in an attempt to deflect the blame elsewhere, suggested the real problem was the high cost of local elevator fees (even though this "direct to U.S." business would by-pass the elevator altogether!). He tried to sell them on the concept that one seller (the CWB) to many buyers would generate better returns to producers as opposed to many sellers to many buyers. The CWB continued to live in a make-believe world of economics in order to preserve their lack of transparency and, in doing so, deflect any accountability.

One of the WBGA directors attending the Winnipeg meeting in 1992 was Ron Hierath, an Alberta wheat farmer who had been legally exporting wheat experimentally alongside Spencer and his barley. Hierath's response after the meeting with the CWB was frank. "The more you examine this whole process, the more ludicrous it becomes from the standpoint of the grain farmer. We are there to serve regulations rather than regulations to serve us, it appears to me. My answer is to be able to market through the Wheat Board, if I wish, and not, if I wish. It has to be optional."

Nearly two years later it looked like Spencer, Hierath and many other independently-minded farmers were going to get their wish.

[16] *Alberta's Minister of Agriculture in 1992.*

Continental Barley Market (1993)

PEANUTS is a familiar cartoon strip to most. An on-going theme was Lucy's placement of a football awaiting Charlie Brown's kick, and her inevitable yank of the ball just as he is about to fulfill his dream.

Time and time again he was lured into believing the next attempt would yield a different result but, alas, she yanked it away at the last minute. This cartoon icon in many ways reflects the numerous attempts by the WBGA to introduce change, the expectation of positive results and the disappointments and rejections along the way.

Eventually, Lucy capitulates, allowing Charlie to kick the ball, but it took cartoonist Charles Schulz a few decades to make it happen. Similarly, it took several decades for the WBGA to "kick their ball" as well. The famous comic strip holds an all too painful kinship to market freedom (the football) and the barley growers (Charlie Brown). Just like Charlie, the WBGA did, finally, connect with their goal, but not before a few yanked away footballs of their own.

In August 1993, federal Agriculture Minister Charlie Mayer rolled up his sleeves and acted on barley. After considerable pressure from the WBGA, the ABC and other like-minded groups, as well as his own Round Table consultations and a commissioned study by Dr. Colin Carter, he instituted the new Continental Barley Market (CBM) by order-in-council. This action allowed farmers and private traders to ship barley directly to U.S. markets without CWB restrictions or intervention — just as Buck Spencer had been advocating. No Export Permits, no buy-backs, no involvement whatsoever from the CWB just as if it were a domestic sale to a feed buyer. What followed was the release of a pent-up flurry of activity, negotiations and deals between large and small Canadian grain companies and feed lots and feed mills across northern and western American states. The North American Free Trade Agreement (NAFTA) had opened the door[17] for this non-tariff business and both grain companies and farmers revelled in the opportunity to create shipments and cash flow in a here-to-fore

[17] *There's that "open door" again...*

dormant trading channel. This was incontrovertible evidence of a new market for Canadian grain and proof positive Canadian farmers could secure expanded marketing options.

Despite the CBM's overwhelming initial success, the Saskatchewan Wheat Pool, joined by the Alberta and Manitoba Pools and assisted by the CWB, was successful in over-ruling Mayer's Order by a court ruling stipulating the action was unconstitutional. This judgement shut down the CBM after 41 days. The CWB quickly stepped in and assumed all the private business conducted in those previous 41 days leaving both buyers and sellers to resolve any offsetting contractual commitments made to fill these deals. For many, it was a financial catastrophe. For the CWB it was a nuisance to unwind, but critical in retaining their monopoly and continuing market power.

Mayer, thinking he had time once the upcoming federal election was over to recover market freedom for farmers, delayed removing barley completely from the CWB's monopoly, as he had done with oats. When the Conservative Party all but disappeared in that unprecedented 1993 election, the Liberals refused to address the topic and the new Minister of Agriculture, Ralph Goodale, steadfastly prevented any meaningful conversation or change to the CWB monopoly.

There were farmers in the United States who opposed the new legislation as well and made their feelings known to state officials. The CWB was viewed as a subsidizing agency designed to support exports by Western Canadian farmers. Any shipment of grain from Canada into the United States was unacceptable to farmers along the border states of North Dakota, Montana and Idaho. Art Froehlich, Alberta Pool's country operations manager at the time recalls the push-back. "Senator Byron Dorgan from North Dakota was quoted as saying if the Canadians tried to ship subsidized grain into the United States, he just might have to turn some of their ballistic missiles towards this possible new invasion problem. We figured he wasn't serious, but it was still a pretty harsh reaction."

With the court order, the U.S. border was once again closed to sales and shipments of barley to anyone other than the CWB. This business volume would never have materialized without the perseverance of the WBGA and the private sector lobbying for change. Grain traders made contacts, established relationships, and instituted credit terms in anticipation of a new market for Canadian feed grains. But it was not to be.

The Board took over all feed barley trades to the United States becoming the principal to all deals entered into by private traders. Canadian export statistics show shipments of feed and malt barley to the United States jumped tenfold thanks to the transactions that took place in those 41 days. They ballooned from 180,000 tonnes in 1992/93 to 1.8 million tonnes in 1993/94. Back under CWB control, continuing business to the United States dropped precipitously over the ensuing years, until feed barley exports approached zero again in 1998. Meanwhile, select malt barley business plateaued at those 1993/94 levels. The new market for Canadian exports had been lost; but perhaps "ignored" is a better description.

Concurrently, exports of Canadian barley to other international destinations began to decline in 1993 as well. From 3.7 million tonnes in 1993, exports dropped steadily reaching their lowest levels during the drought of 2002 at 317,000 tonnes. From 2002 to 2012, annual exports averaged 1.5 million tonnes, a sad outcome for all Western Canadian barley farmers. The entire market for Canadian barley had effectively disappeared. International buyers for Canadian feed barley were not pursued by the CWB resulting in higher inventories languishing in prairie bins, depressing prices for the only remaining market, the domestic feeders. The CWB didn't understand the feed barley market in Canada or abroad and had little interest in pursuing it — to the detriment to Canadian barley farmers.

What looked like a major victory for farmers in their efforts to attain the freedom of dual markets for barley and, potentially, wheat, turned into yet another discouraging loss. Stronger measures were necessary which would entail a costly and protracted legal battle which became known as the Charter Challenge. This action was favoured by some members of the WBGA while others considered taking matters into their own hands by way of a more confrontational, highly visible public undertaking — the Border Crossing. These were the next milestones on the road to market freedom.

Charter Challenge (1993)

1993 was a tough year for barley farmers. Not only did they lose the opportunity to fulfill their dream of market freedom through the new Continental Barley Market when it failed, they also lost their political ally in the federal Progressive Conservative Party when it lost their majority government in the election in October of that year. Power reverted back to the Liberals after the Mulroney years and a brief appointment of Kim Campbell. All doors seemed to be closing in on each and every effort they undertook to remove what they considered to be the largest barrier to their success — the CWB monopoly.

Tired of the CWB's apparent apathy towards barley marketing and mindful of John Channon's words suggesting "someone should take the CWB to court to challenge their authority" the WBGA shifted their focus to the courts in October 1993. They joined forces as plaintiffs with the Alberta Barley Commission and twenty-one individual farmers across the Prairies in a lawsuit against the Canadian government and the Wheat Board. Together this group launched a Class Action Suit which challenged the CWB Act under the Canadian Charter of Rights and Freedoms.

The Canadian Charter of Rights and Freedoms had been indoctrinated in 1982 as part of Canada's Constitution. It is intended to protect every Canadian's right to be treated equally under the law. The Charter guarantees broad equality rights and other fundamental rights such as the freedom of expression, freedom of assembly and freedom of religion.

The Charter sets out those rights and freedoms Canadians believe are necessary in a free and democratic society and, as a document, it makes up one part of the Canadian Constitution. The Constitution is the supreme law of Canada; all other laws must be consistent with the rules set out in it. If they are not, they may not be valid. Since the Charter is part of the Constitution, it is the most important law we have in Canada. However, the rights and freedoms in the Charter are not absolute and, as such, may require legal interpretation and in some cases, judicial rulings.

The claim of the barley group's lawsuit asked the court to declare the Wheat Board Act, or certain parts of it, unconstitutional and having no legal force and effect, because it compromised three guarantees to all Canadians included in the Charter. The sections of the Charter they identified and intended to pursue were:

1. Freedom of choice in association
2. Freedom in the pursuit of one's livelihood
3. Freedom from discrimination based on geographic location

The claimants' lawyers felt all three of these rights were being impacted negatively and their challenge was both applicable and defensible in court. In simple terms and wording, the thrust of the claimants' presentation was as follows:

a) The government brought about the CWB single desk selling system to serve its own interests (war, international grain agreements and foreign policy), not to benefit western grain producers.

b) The fact that Canadians are more peaceful and producers have tolerated the CWB monopoly until recent years should not be mistaken for their support for it or that this anomaly to freedom should be tolerated indefinitely, in defiance of reason, good sense and the freedoms guaranteed under the Charter.

c) Whatever "premiums" commanded by the CWB in international markets are negligible at best, and in any event don't flow through to producers.

d) The Canadian grain handling system, of which the CWB is a major player, is so inefficient that gains from the CWB system, if any, are eaten up.

e} Even the limited form of dual marketing system experienced to date has not proven that such would not work to the benefit of producers.

Exactly three years later, on October 15, 1996, the challenge finally made its way to the federal court system in Calgary after a year of technical wrangling over the pleadings, seven pre-trial hearings, over 4,000 pages of live testimony heard over four weeks before the trial justice, 16 written legal arguments and 14 binders full of legal precedents.

Six Western Canadian farmers described how the actions, or lack of action, on the part of the Canadian Wheat Board negatively impacted their farming businesses. They described their farming practices, cash flow requirements, special crop diversification and the marketing function of these crops in comparison to Board grains. Other testimony was provided by industry, market analysts and academics, all supporting the position presented by the ABC and fellow claimants in the challenge.

Several witnesses spoke in opposition to the challenge. One of those witnesses was National Farmers Union (NFU) President and CEO, Nettie Wiebe. Her testimony appeared to carry disproportionate weight with Judge J. Muldoon, the judge presiding over the case, given she was not a significantly large barley farmer. According to Brian Otto, who attended the proceedings every single day, "The judge was more enamored with her academic credentials and bias towards the Canadian Wheat Board than the mountain of testimony from those witnesses who spoke in support of the challenge."

The actual proceedings took four weeks to complete in Calgary and then in Winnipeg, capping off those three years of preparation and expenses in the process. All that remained was a decision by the judge — right? Not so fast buck-o!

Finally, in May 1997, Justice Muldoon, delivered his verdict. He made a specific note of the fact the issue before the court is "not what is best for all farmers, or who or how many farmers dislike the monopoly, but whether Parliament's chosen instrument infringes on the plaintiff's Charter rights." He believed Parliament, not farmers or the court should decide what is best in economic terms for all of Canada and Canadians and, in his judgement, a mandatory CWB is in our national interest.

To the specific points, the judge ruled that farmers aren't required to associate with other producers but, rather, that all producers do the same thing — sell their export wheat and barley to the CWB. No law is preventing them from growing wheat and barley. Specifically, farmers are not forced to associate with the Crown marketing agency — only your grain is! The claimants felt this position was splitting hairs, but often that's what rulings come down to in the courts. In his ruling Judge Muldoon stated, "The farmers' association with the CWB is centered around purely economic interests, which are not protected under the Charter."

Regarding the pursuit of one's livelihood, the CWB does not prevent anyone from earning a livelihood. Neither the right to work or property rights are protected under the Charter, only the right to try and earn a living. These are the laws of the land and if a farmer doesn't like the stipulations inside the CWB's Designated Area, he is free to move elsewhere. Let's repeat that for clarity — "He is free to move elsewhere."

The last point, "freedom from discrimination based on geographic location" was also unfounded in the judge's eyes. The CWB Act does not "negatively impact their fundamental human dignity or freedom."

In summary, Judge Muldoon expressed concern that, "should this case succeed and kill the CWB, government couldn't re-create control over trade in the future even if that was their desire." He believed that government should be able to do as they wish; decide what's best for Canada no matter what farmers themselves want. The CWB markets grain in an "orderly manner"[18] and that allows them to override individual farmer's rights.

While the judge admitted the CWB may not be the best means of marketing Western Canadian grain and further admitted some of its operations are unfair[19], this is a political problem, not a Charter one. In his learned opinion, Parliament must be free to regulate the market as it sees fit. The CWB is an instrument of the State, used to do just that.

Muldoon added "If the plaintiffs don't like the CWB monopoly they should vote for a party that will change it." (Hold on to that thought). He added "While the Wheat Board is arguably not responsible or so efficient as some producers desire, the evidence has shown that it achieves its objectives."

After three years of commitment to the case, this ruling was a disappointing and disheartening outcome both in terms of the ruling and in terms of faith in the judicial system. What would appear to be an open-and-shut case went against them. Their only remaining option was to take their case to the Supreme Court of Canada and hope for their case to be heard there.

WBGA President Doug Robertson explains what happened after the Muldoon judgement. "The Charter Challenge against the CWB monopoly dragged on until 2001 when we were denied Supreme Court appeal of the original 1997 ruling which said basically that because Canadians have no property rights, farmers have no Charter right to own their own grain and thus decide their own marketing system for wheat and barley. The Government of Canada has the right to decide what is in the "best interests of Canada" and can change the system or not if they choose to."

The loss was devastating for the plaintiffs. Thousands of hours and $1.2 million in funding from the Alberta Barley Commission had been dedicated to the challenge. Losing was one thing, but to be told, as a farmer, you don't own the grain you toiled to produce is unfathomable. Remember, this only applies to wheat and barley on the prairies. There are different sets of rules for non-CWB grains and crops produced outside Western

[18] *Author's Note – Whatever "orderly manner" meant?*

[19] *WBGA insert - burdensome buyback costs, unfair storage and handling costs, loss of local value adding, adding dockage in at terminals and charging farmers for unnecessary cleaning.*

Canada. If this isn't a broken system of unbalanced and egregious laws, what is? It was also regrettable to see that $1.2 million of farmer money spent with no result. It could have been allocated to so many other important areas.

The political climate had also turned against the WBGA during the course of the Challenge. When they launched the legal action in 1993, the Progressive Conservative Party held a majority government in Ottawa with 169 of 295 federal seats. The federal election in October 1993 resulted in the PC's retaining only 2 of those 169 seats. It was the worst electoral defeat in Canadian parliamentary history, and it wasn't until 2006 and a convergence of the Progressive Conservative and Reform parties that the Conservatives were able to form a government once again. It took another five years before they were able to gain majority in parliament. In the intervening 13 years the Liberal Party formed the government, mostly with their own majority or a Bloc Québécois coalition. The significance of this parliamentary structure was quite simple. The Liberal party had zero interest in diminishing or removing the powers of the CWB. It wasn't a topic for discussion — full stop.

The Charter Challenge had failed, and the sympathetic ear of the Progressive Conservative Party was gone. The fledgling Reform Party aligned with the WBGA and other open-minded farm groups in Western Canada but, aside from making a stir in the House of Commons, had little influence on agriculture policy. Importantly, farmers in Western Canada, along with many other Canadians, took Justice Muldoon's suggestion to heart and "voted for another party"[20], but it took some time.

The Border Crossing (1996)

WBGA farmers are not criminals, far from it actually. For 20 years they worked as an organization within the regulations of Canada's Customs laws and the CWB Act. But progress wasn't happening, marketing freedom lessened, if that was possible, and frustration and debt continued to mount due to the poor performance of the CWB as the single agent for export barley sales.

The members of the WGBA were exasperated and exhausted. The CWB's unwillingness to act on the feed barley opportunity in Idaho presented to them by Buck Spencer and Herb Allen, and the lack of follow through on the obvious interest in Canadian feed barley discovered during the Continental Market's short 41 day window created a boiling point for some and the desire to push a little harder. In that year the Charter Challenge was still in the courts, but it looked

[20] *Right leaning parties gained ground in subsequent elections after the 1993 rout of 54 seats. They won 80 seats in 1997, 78 in 2000, 99 in 2004, 124 in 2006 (forming the government), 143 in 2008 and finally a majority in 2011 with 166 seats.*

like it would be a long time working its way through. In the meantime, barley inventories languished, and markets remained depressed.

It was no surprise then, in 1996, when the gloves finally came off and farmers took matters into their own hands. They decided a public demonstration of some sort was necessary.

They knew there would be a price to pay for their actions — not only in the cost of the endeavour but possibly too in the court of public opinion. Taking the government to court was one thing but targeting the CWB in the class action suit pitted farmer against farmer, not the best of scenarios. However, if they could draw broader public attention to their cause, the consensus was it would be worth it. The courts were unsympathetic, and the Liberal government was completely deaf to their requests. Not even demands, just requests — at least so far.

A strategic plan evolved. On April 26, 1996, a group of farmers gathered at Alberta's Coutts/Sweetgrass Canada Customs border crossing intending to transport grain into the United States without CWB Export Permits as required. The decision to break a law was not taken lightly by these farmers, but months earlier one brave Manitoban farmer, Andy McMechan, led the way with his own rebellious act of defiance. His action and personal sacrifice deserved support from other farmers. McMechan had been charged with "failing to keep the peace" after he hauled some wheat and barley across the Canada/USA border in Manitoba and refused to surrender his tractor as ordered by Canada Customs officials. McMechan was also charged with shipping grain into the United States without an Export Permit. His fines totaled $33,000 and he was ordered to pay the CWB $55,000 in compensation. McMechan also spent 155 days in jail and was treated as a hardened life-long criminal while incarcerated.

"They don't pay any of our fertilizer bills, yet they own the grain soon as it's grown," Mr. Russell Barrows, a Coutts, Alberta farmer said when he saw pictures of Mr. McMechan being led into court in shackles, he nearly wept "to think this is going on in Canada."

The Agricultural Economics branch of the Alberta government had been monitoring the movement of grain into the United States for the past 2-3 years and had even encouraged some farmers to do so legally in order to track the process and create a cost comparison of the transactions. Buck Spencer concluded several transactions and provided this information to the provincial government which was subsequently shared with all farmers in the WBGA's "The Barley Grower" newsletters.

But this time around there weren't any permits or CWB buy-backs — just a will to defy the CWB and the laws of the land to test the system and create some public awareness. How far would this legislation go to impede the sale and shipment of their own grain to new markets?

Word travelled through the WBGA and the date and time were chosen. Enough farmers made the commitment to participate, and with that, the plan was struck. The Alberta government was alerted, as were Canada Border Services and the media. This wasn't meant to catch authorities off guard, it was designed to bring the issue to a head.

Thirteen farmers showed up in Coutts, Alberta prepared to cross the border with their grain. Quantities varied from a full B-train truck load

Source: CBC News

to a single bag of wheat. In a creative display of symbolism the conveyances included large and small trucks, a wheelbarrow and even one farmer who carried a single bag across on foot.

The farmers weren't alone in their defiance. Many supporters joined them to witness the event and provide much needed encouragement. Richard Nordstrom was one of those witnesses. He drove from his farm near Viking to observe the events and acted as the on-going communications conduit to government. "I talked to the government guys on and off all day," Richard recalls. "We told them what was happening and got advice on how we should handle different obstacles."

Another WBGA member, Rick Strankman, was there too, planning to cross with a few bags of grain. "A lot of the grain we took across was donated to a local 4H club," Strankman recalls. "It wasn't about the money; it was about the principle." But he almost didn't make it into the United States at all, for a totally unrelated matter. As border agents reviewed farmers' identification it was discovered there was an outstanding warrant for Strankman for an unpaid traffic ticket. Who knew you couldn't cross the border if you owed the government $50? One of the RCMP told him to come with him in his cruiser (which caused Rick some mild concern). They got in the officer's car and he drove to Milk River. The officer had called ahead to alert a local judge. She issued Strankman with a "Promise to Appear" notice and they promptly returned to the border in time for him to cross with the others. "The RCMP and Customs employees at the border were really great," recalls Strankman. "They sympathized with us and were very helpful in making this work for us. After all, we hadn't broken any laws — not yet at least."

Buck Spencer had his own encounter with authorities that spring day. When he arrived at the border crossing, he noticed two guards on an elevated platform. They were armed with rifles which seemed more than a little extreme to Spencer. Canada Customs had been informed farmers would be conducting a rather public display at the crossing so they really didn't know what to expect and they certainly didn't want it to turn violent. But the encounter with the farmers was jovial and friendly. No one was there to fight.

Spencer was still concerned armed guards might create the wrong kind of optics for the media on a peaceful protest that day so he moved his truck into the nearby Freightways parking lot and got out his camera and telescopic lens. "I made a lot of fuss to make sure they saw me close by, then I rested my elbows on the hood of my truck and pointed the camera at the guards on the platform," says Spencer. "They watched me for a while and, finally, they got the hell out of there! The funny thing was I forgot to put film in the camera — but they didn't know that."

Mike Leslie, past ABC General Manager recalls the events of the day in Coutts, Alberta. He knew of the building frustration amongst barley farmers and of their plans to elevate the message to gain some public attention.

"There were better and more diplomatic ways to get the message across," he noted. "But certainly nothing quite as impactful and newsworthy."

Once clear of the border, the convoy headed south to Shelby, Montana for the evening. Some of the grain was scheduled for delivery nearby the following day. The event brought with it mixed emotions from various American groups. U.S. feeders were happy to see another possible source of feed grain entering their market, while U.S. farmers saw this as more competition — and subsidized at that! They viewed the CWB as a marketing board that kept export prices low and subsidized farmers through government support. From their perspective this was a contravention of the NAFTA trade agreement and a threat to their livelihoods.

Richard Nordstrom recalls an incident where Omar Broughton, a representative of the Alberta provincial government at the time, got roughed up a little bit by some locals while in Montana. "He was along for the trip taking pictures and recording the event for the government. No one down south knew who he was, but they took exception to him taking pictures and unceremoniously shoved him back in his car, threw his camera in the back seat and told him to get moving. He was a little unsettled by the altercation but otherwise okay and he joined us for dinner. But it was clear not everyone in the U.S. was happy to see us."

Richard had huge compliments for the owner of the Dixie Inn in Shelby. "There were about 40 of us for dinner and we set it up in advance to make sure he would be ready for us. He treated us really well. We all had big steak dinners and spent a great evening together discussing the day and how good we all felt about doing something symbolic and memorable."

The evening had its own drama thanks to a fellow who "didn't look like he belonged with the group" according to Rick Strankman. "He certainly wasn't a farmer. Turns out he was a CBC reporter who had infiltrated the group and was trying to nose his way around to get a story. We didn't appreciate his deceit," recalled Strankman. "I was all for grabbing him by the collar and helping him find the front door quickly. But Richard cooled me down and looked after it!"

No U.S. laws were broken bringing Canadian grain into the United States as an Import Permit was not required, so the convoy was able to enter the country without incident. But the real problems surfaced upon their return to Canada. The RCMP were waiting for them and all 13 farmers were arrested, their vehicles were seized at the border and the "lawbreakers" were all processed. In an attempt to draw attention to the absurdity of the whole situation Buck Spencer intervened with his own suggestion that all wheelbarrows and shoes worn by these desperadoes should also be seized. Apparently, there is no room for humour at Canada Customs. If he hadn't known some of the agents personally, he might have found himself up on charges for crimes against the nation too.

As the day of their return wore on, the farmers quickly realized the border guards had issued orders seizing their trucks, which left them wondering how they were going to get home. But the border guards had a rather fatal flaw in their plan—no one had actually seized their keys. The farmers quietly wandered outside, got in their trucks and drove away. Unfortunately, when the border agents realized what was happening, they alerted the RCMP who caught up to the trucks and pulled them over. The farmers were ticketed for taking their trucks from the Canada Customs parking lot after they had been seized.

The penalties[21] faced by the 13 Alberta farmers who were charged for taking their grain[22] over the U.S. border included:

Gary Brandt — Age 33, of Viking, faced 62 days in jail. He took a bag of wheat across the border, forgot about it and ended up carrying it back into Canada.

Ron Duffy — Age 50, from Lacombe, faced 68 days in jail. He took one bag across the border, then a commercial quantity of wheat.

Jim Chatenay — Age 59, from Penhold, faced 62 days in jail. He took a bushel of wheat to the U.S. and donated it to a 4-H club.

Martin Hall — Age 42, from Vulcan, faced 131 days in jail. He took a semi-trailer full of wheat across the border and sold it.

Rod Hanger — Age 32, from Three Hills, faced 75 days in jail. He took a commercial load of wheat across the border and sold it.

Noel Hyslip — Age 42, from Vulcan, faced 131 days in jail. He took a semi-trailer full of wheat across the border and sold it.

Ike Lanier — Age 72, from Lethbridge, faced 60 days in jail. He trucked 300 bushels across the border.

Bill Moore — Age 63, from Red Deer, faced 131 days in jail. He donated a bag of wheat to a 4-H Club, then took a half-ton truck of wheat across the border.

Jim Ness — Age 58, from New Brigden, faced 25 days in jail. He drove 100 lbs. of barley across the border and donated it to the 4-H Club.

Mark Peterson — Age 42, from Cereal, faced 124 days in jail. He hauled a truckload of wheat across the border.

---

[21] *No one could explain why the fines varied from one farmer to another. It wasn't related to the quantity of grain they transported.*

[22] *Most farmers hauled wheat across the border because it was easier to find a home for small lots of wheat than barley in the area. And this was a challenge to the Canadian "Wheat" Board after all.*

Rick Strankman — Age 49, from Altario, faced 180 days in jail. He took 756 bushels of wheat across the border and sold it for $1.50 per bushel higher than the Canadian price.

John Turcato — Age 42, from Taber, faced 131 days in jail. He drove 900 bushels of barley across the border.

Darren Winczura — Age 35, from Viking, faced 24 days in jail. He drove a bag of wheat across the border.

Six years later, the 13 farmers faced a judge in Lethbridge. The emotions ahead of the actual trial ranged from jubilation to trepidation as the charged farmers faced rulings along with possible fines and even incarceration. They were ready to go to jail to make their point, but that thought brought with it another set of personal issues and concerns.

The local news covered the events of the day and the personal conviction of the 13 farmers charged.

LETHBRIDGE, Alta., Oct 31, 2002 (The Canadian Press via COMTEX) — Thirteen Alberta farmers who broke customs rules by taking their grain over the border were taken to jail Thursday as their wives and children broke down in tears and hundreds more — including Premier Ralph Klein — rallied in protest.

The cheering, clapping protesters formed a human corridor to block traffic and allow the 13 and their families to walk into the courthouse, where the farmers gave themselves up to security staff. The first two were handcuffed but the rest were not after Canadian Alliance MP Art Hanger, whose nephew Rod is among the 13, intervened to ask, "Are the handcuffs really necessary?"

The 13 said little while they were processed and taken away.

Noel Hyslip, a 42-year-old farmer from Vulcan, paused for a last good-bye to his wife and three children. He kissed his teary nine-year-old daughter Erin on the cheek and whispered in her ear: "I love you." He said he shared his children's pain and confusion. "I can't understand it so I can't see how they can," he said, tears filling his eyes. "It's hard to believe you're in Canada"

They face paying fines ranging between $1,000 and $7,500 or staying in jail for terms ranging from just under a month to half a year. Earlier Thursday, about 500 placard-waving farmers from as far away as Manitoba and Montana rallied outside the courthouse to protest the Canadian Wheat Board policies that dictate they sell their grain to the board instead of trying for a better price through independent marketing.

Many carried signs bearing slogans such as: Why do Eastern Farmers Have a Choice? We Don't! and The Canadian Wheat Board is a Monopoly. One woman wore prison stripes and a ball and chain. Musicians played guitars and sang about life on the farm.

Lindsay Hall, 12, of Vulcan, Alta., said she understood why her father Martin was willing to go to jail

Alberta farmers jailed for violating custom rules by hauling grain to U.S.

for more than four months. "I'm going to miss him but I know that he's doing the right thing because it isn't fair that they can't sell their grain to whoever they want," she said. Many wives said it will be the longest time they've ever spent apart from their husbands. "This is really hard on me," said Martin's wife, Marty. He'll be in jail for their 14th wedding anniversary.

Those going to jail are members of Farmers for Justice, a coalition of grain farmers who want the option to market their own barley and wheat. In 1996, they were charged under the Canada Customs Act for illegally transporting grain across the U.S. border because they didn't have proper export documents. At the time, Canadian farmers were fetching $8.50 Cdn a bushel for durum wheat south of the border, instead of $3.50 from the wheat board.

The farmers claim they are being discriminated against because their counterparts in Ontario and Quebec are allowed to market their own products, but farmers in Alberta, Saskatchewan and Manitoba have to sell their barley and wheat to the board.

Klein told the rally that the prison terms show the system is not working. "Today Alberta farmers will face punishment for doing what farmers are supposed to do and that's to raise, harvest and sell their crops," Klein said as the crowd cheered. "When decent, hardworking Alberta farmers are willing to take the extreme measure of going to jail for the sake of fundamental freedoms that other businesses take for granted, there is something wrong with the laws of the land."

In Ottawa, Canadian Alliance Leader Stephen Harper and Tory Leader Joe Clark also criticized the *federal Liberals for the marketing rules they say are unfair to western farmers. But Ralph Goodale, the federal minister responsible for the wheat board, said the board enjoys wide support from farmers. He suggested the jailed 13 were grandstanding. "They have been seeking to maximize their publicity in this matter and that is their right. But let's be clear — the choice, with respect to the jail proceedings, was one that was chosen by them."*

Ken Ritter, the wheat board chairman, urged the farmers to pay the fines "and return home to their families." Ritter defended the wheat board's single-desk marketing model. By having the board combine and sell the farmers' grain as one unit, it can command top dollar in the world market, he said.

But the organization still had several Montana farmers, who drove north for the rally, shaking their heads. "It's a sad day in history for Canadians," said Ron Jensen, from Shelby, Montana. "You can't put the people who grow the food you eat in jail."

But they did. The circumstances surrounding this protest are noteworthy as is the central issue of individual rights, an important cause for all farmers.

The Farmer Perspective

Noel Hyslip

"After years of lobbying the government for reform, only to achieve complicated marketing options still through the single desk, in the spring of 1996, the decision was made by myself and several other Alberta farmers to export a 25-kilogram sack of barley and donate it to the Montana 4-H Club. It was intended as a demonstration to show the power the government held over farmers.

Alberta farmers Jim Ness, left, Noel Hyslip and Rick Strankman

Upon our return to the Canadian border, we found a large increase in staff at the Canada Customs crossing, as well as several members of the Royal Canadian Mounted Police.

After a few hours of peacefully processing our paperwork, we were charged with exporting grain without a Canadian Wheat Board permit, which carried a penalty of 45 days in jail, and we had our vehicles seized.

For six, long stress-filled years, we were hauled in and out of courtrooms only to find out that we were guilty. Even though we had all the time, effort and cost of producing that crop, it wasn't ours to even give away.

On Oct. 31, 2002, with the harvest unfinished and the crop still laying in the field, and with family, friends and hundreds of farmers looking on in disbelief, I, along with 12 others, turned ourselves into the Lethbridge courthouse, where we were put in handcuffs and leg chains, placed in the back of a van and hauled to the provincial correctional centre in Lethbridge. It is a process that haunts me to this day."

Rick Strankman

"It all got very real inside the Lethbridge correctional center," recalls Strankman. "It was a sobering moment to be put in the same shoes as Manitoba farmer Andy McMechan, who spent 155 days in jail with similar charges. No one can anticipate the feeling of those cold, hard steel bars until you clasp them from inside a small jail cell. We all owe a great debt of gratitude to Andy who made the personal sacrifice to stand by his (and our) beliefs."

John Turcato

John Turcato, a 42-year-old cattle and grain farmer from Taber who spent 34 days in jail to pay off his fines, said he hopes this high-profile protest might have some influence on the election results. "I think it opened up a lot of eyes and we got a lot more response than we ever thought that we would get," he said.

Ron Duffy

"We just want them to realize that this is not going away," says the 50-year-old grain farmer from Lacombe. "This is not the end of the fight. This is the beginning of a bigger one."

After the border crossing incident at Coutts, and Andy McMechan's arrest in Manitoba, two signs on the main north/south highways showed up welcoming visitors to Canada. They read:

The signs were posted by disgruntled farmers upset with the treatment of fellow farmers and the heavy-handed reaction by the federal government in dealing with (or not dealing with) the problem.

Jim Chatenay

One WBGA member, Jim Chatenay of Penhold, Alta., faced time in jail for donating a bushel of wheat to a 4-H club in Montana. Jim was also one of 10 elected directors on the Canadian Wheat Board but, unlike his peers at the CWB, he believed farmers should have the choice to market their grain independently of the board. He said, "Many people in the West are furious because farmers in Ontario and Quebec can market their own products, while those on the Prairies have to sell barley and wheat to the Canadian Wheat Board."

"To me, that's not fair," Chatenay told CBC Newsworld on Thursday, as the deadline to pay his $2,000 fine expired. He was facing 62 days in jail. "What we really believe in is that in one part of the country we jail farmers for selling their grain ... and in other parts of the country they are allowed to sell their grain without going to jail," Chatenay said. "To me, that is discrimination."

In a diary Jim kept during his incarceration he offered a factual account of the group's time in jail. He made the following notes...

"At the courthouse they took us to a holding area and took our wallets and belts and gave us leg irons, chains or whatever you call it, and two of us were handcuffed together. Then we were taken by an armoured-looking car to the facility, where we were supplied with jail garb. They give you privacy to change into the coveralls. Most of my fellow farmers had already put theirs on — I was about second to last and put mine on backwards. They got a kick out of that. You have to make your own fun when you're stressed.

You're not allowed anything of your own — socks, shorts, they provide everything, even toothpaste. The beds are hard, the pillows are like leather and only an inch thick. The meals so far have been pretty good. The guards are exceptionally kind and sympathetic. Two of them had tears in their eyes — they come from farm backgrounds — and the other inmates can't believe what's happened to us. I guess we're something new and special in this joint.

I'm bunking with Ron Duffy. They have us two to a cell and we have two blankets each. Breakfast was at 7. We had porridge, a glass of juice and a couple of slices of toast. Lunch was grilled cheese sandwiches. Last night was a great meal — pasta with roast chicken, kind of like Swiss Chalet. They are accommodating us in every way.

My biggest issue was my wife worrying about me and about where I was. I tried to call her today but I think she's gone shopping. I'll get hold of her later. For 40 years she's been trying to get me to wear coveralls, so she'll be happy to see me now.

The good news is that I got 40 days off my sentence of 62 days so I'll be out Nov. 23. The longest anyone will stay in here is Dec. 3, so we'll all be home for Christmas. They have a formula that applies to everybody. You can get time off for community service and so forth. The feeling among some is that we told our story. Me, I want to be in here. I don't need to chop down a tree at my age. I'm almost 60.

So far we've been separate from the general population but we're getting some new guys in our section tonight. These guys, other inmates, are OK. I'm not worried about it.

Our meals are brought to us. We have a rumpus room/dining room type of area, about 40 by 25 feet, with five tables. Our cells are just down the hallway. My cell is Number 5. I've got a view toward the road. I see the sunrise every morning but that's about it. The bars are real thick. It's going well, although the air's a little stale. You can't open the window."

The story of the 13 farmers charged during this event has become legend in the years to follow. Their commitment in their belief and self sacrifice in following through has not been forgotten by Western Canadian farmers. It was also not lost on the politicians who bore some responsibility for their inaction. Their story doesn't end here, but we have to save some parts for a happy ending.

Alberta Government Action

CHOICE MATTERS

Marketing choice supports economic opportunity. April 2004

FOR SALE

OPEN GRAIN MARKETS IN ALBERTA

A vision for the future where innovation, entrepreneurship, and risk management are rewarded.

Following the 2002 trial and conviction of the farmers who crossed the Canada-USA border in 1996, the Alberta government took more assertive action. Led by Minister of Agriculture, Shirley McClellan and backed by Premier Ralph Klein, they took a stand — a stand for market freedom.

"Choice Matters" became a regular publication of the provincial government with the sole purpose of pressuring Ottawa and supporters of the CWB to modernize their thinking and accept the dual market option as proposed by the WBGA and others. Klein's government recognized the importance of agriculture to the Alberta economy and the need for incentive and innovation.

In the inaugural publication, Deputy Premier and Minister of Agriculture Shirley McClellan made the following statements:

"OPEN GRAIN MARKETS IN ALBERTA"

A vision for the future where innovation, entrepreneurship, and risk management are rewarded.

Alberta's grain farmers are an intelligent bunch.

They know what it takes to grow a good crop — and how to choose seed, fertilizer and pesticide.

They know how to time seeding and spraying and harvest. They're responsible for the $2-billion provincial crop industry.

They also know how to manage their risk, and they know what their customers want.

Finally, they know that in order to capitalize on and compete in today's global markets and domestic opportunities, they need marketing choice.

The Alberta government sees the great potential of this industry, but we also see what stands in the way. For the agriculture industry to grow into the future, the Canadian Wheat Board should be one option for marketing wheat and barley — not the only option.

This first issue of CHOICE MATTERS IS ABOUT THE Alberta government's vision for the future of the grain industry, a vision shared by many Albertans. We see a marketing system where innovation, entrepreneurship, and risk management are rewarded...where individual producers decide what is best for their individual operations.

I hope that what your read in CHOICE MATTERS will promote the discussion in order to discover new ways and better solutions — this is a topic we all need to talk about. This is your industry and your choice. Make your voice heard.

Shirley McClellan

Grain Growers of Canada

There's strength in unity and benefit of collaboration for groups with similar needs. By their nature, farmers are independent and self sufficient and that works fine for choices in lifestyle and managing the farm. But it's not an effective choice when it comes to matters of systemic change and progressive movements. For that to happen individuals need to act in a more collective, collaborative manner surrounding themselves with peers and developing unified fronts. This approach had become crystal clear to the WBGA after numerous attempts acting on their own had failed to accomplish their goal of marketing freedom.

In June 2000, the WBGA joined in a collaborative approach with other farm organizations across Canada to form the Grain Growers of Canada (GGC). The GGC was established to counteract the influence of the Canadian Federation of Agriculture in ag policy and provide support for grain and oilseed producers who were unrepresented until then. Collectively these groups were now able to speak as a single voice representing a broader geography and commodity base.

Numerous grain and oilseed organizations were involved in its founding:

- Alberta Barley Commission (ABC)
- Atlantic Grains Council (AGC)
- British Columbia Grain Producers Association (BCGPA)
- Canadian Canola Growers Association (CCGA)
- Fédération des Producteurs de Cultures Commerciales du Québec (FPCCQ)

- Manitoba Corn Growers Association (MCGA)
- Ontario Corn Producers' Association (OCPA)
- Ontario Soybean Growers (OSG)
- Ontario Wheat Producers Marketing Board (OWPMB)
- Western Barley Growers Association (WBGA)
- Western Canadian Wheat Growers Association (WCWGA)

The need for representation in Ottawa was quite clear for all these groups and sharing the cost meant all of them could have a presence in Ottawa on a constant basis. "It also meant we had a place to go when we came for meetings and a network of like-minded groups who also benefited from the shared service," says Doug Robertson.

The trips back and forth to Ottawa were getting expensive, and most often the WBGA delegates paid their own way because there wasn't enough money in the bank account to cover expenses. But it was important work, so the directors dug into their own pockets.

The founding principal of the GGC was that participating groups should operate on consensus — agree on the issues that they can agree on and take those forward as policy positions but allow groups that have sensitivity issues to opt out of them. For example, eastern groups who were part of supply managed industries or groups who were part of the Canada Federation of Agriculture found themselves caught between opposing policies and unable to support certain positions.

"The WBGA had good representation on the GGC for a number of years," recalls Robertson. "The advantage of GGC for western wheat and barley groups was the eastern guys used to take little interest in western concerns such as the CWB. 'Why should we care — it doesn't affect us', they would say. But now, we have good support to the point that groups like the Ontario Wheat Producers Marketing Board (OWPMB) will say 'We have freedom to choose our marketing system, why can't prairie farmers?' The disadvantage is that with all umbrella groups, smaller organization member positions may get somewhat diluted or compromised."

Now, in 2022, Grain Growers of Canada has been active for more than 20 years and continues to provide a common voice on many topics of concern to farmers. The WBGA is proud of its initial role in the creation of the GGC and its on-going success as a voice in Ottawa for farmers all across Canada.

WTO Session (2005)

In 2005, the WBGA and other producer-based farm groups headed to Geneva. The occasion was the 10th anniversary of the World Trade Organization and the DOHA Round of negotiations. The views of the WBGA were about to be heard on a global scale at a gathering of important, powerful international trade negotiators. This was easily the highest level "above their weight class" the WBGA had ever entered.

Farmers in Western Canada had limited knowledge about Canada's voice at the WTO or other global agencies on international trade and trade distorting barriers. The CWB was the sole source of information and policy in this process for western farmers executing their same superior claims of "knowing what's best" for these simple prairie farmers. But that was about to change.

"I heard about some WTO meetings on the radio," says Doug McBain. "There was a WTO open house in Geneva for NGO's (non government organizations) and I called Nithi Govindasamy at the Alberta government and told him I thought we should be going to this. And he said "Yes, yes, absolutely yes! Let's do it!" So he, Helmut Mach, Alberta's Director of Trade Policy and Doug Campbell arranged it through Ottawa and we made our first of six trips to Europe to speak on behalf of Western Canadian farmers. We went to Geneva and other world destinations as part of a Canadian agriculture association."

Alberta Agriculture's Trade Policy Advisor, and later Saskatchewan's Associate Deputy Minister of Agriculture, Nithi Govindasamy, was a strong advocate for the WBGA. He believed their message was important and should be heard. He accompanied the WBGA contingent to their first WTO meeting that Doug McBain had alerted him about. "The guys from the WBGA were larger than life," says Govindasamy. "They were visionaries who never gave up. They didn't want to be in the limelight, but they played a huge part in helping guide Canadian ag policy in the 1980's and beyond."

Prior to the mid 1980's, politicians in Eastern Canada paid little attention to western agriculture, particularly cereal grains as that was the domain of the Canadian Wheat Board. Nothing to look at here. They were preoccupied with keeping the supply management sectors happy and this was the singular message from our negotiators at the WTO. Canada was known to oppose the lifting of trade barriers when it threatened supply management or the Canadian Wheat Board.

Western groups like the wheat and barley growers' associations had a different message. They spoke about competition, removal of subsidies and open markets. They began to drive change, bringing important topics to the attention of elected officials. These prairie-based ag groups lobbied for a larger voice for the west, at home and abroad. In Alberta, Provincial Agriculture Ministers Shirley McClellan, followed in that position later by Doug Horner embraced their needs and took up the fight. Together, the provincial government and the WBGA created a greater awareness of the magnitude and importance of ag trade, in particular western grains, on a global scale.

Govindasamy and Mach recognized an opportunity to include this group of local stake-

From the floor of the WTO Symposium meeting in Geneva in 2005 — Doug Robertson

holders in a critical round of talks at the World Trade Organization in Geneva which began in Doha, Qatar in 2001. These on-going discussions became known as the DOHA Round which were particularly important to the meaningful development of free trade and market access with proposed removal of tariffs. The Canadian Wheat Board, along with Canada's supply management programs were the two Canadian topics directly in the cross hairs of this dialogue.

Officially, Canada was ably represented by Agriculture and Agri Food Canada's Chief Agriculture Trade Negotiator, Steve Verheul. It became evident fairly quickly that a group of western Canadian farmers was an unusual contingent to attend the sessions, but the WBGA was well received as they spoke in favour of reduced subsidies and an elimination of the trade-distorting support measures and the elimination of direct and indirect export subsidies resulting from state trading enterprises like the CWB. "Participants at the session were shocked a group from Canada supported free trade," recalls Doug Robertson. "Everything from Canada had been about supply management, but when the WBGA was involved the SM guys didn't say anything."

Representatives from the CWB also attended this round of trade discussions, but it was a huge and unexpected surprise to their senior team to find one of their own Directors there in the ranks of the WBGA. Jim Chatenay had not been invited to attend the sessions on behalf of the CWB but he paid his own way to Geneva and sat with the WBGA contingent. The CWB team had no idea what Jim might say and his position as a CWB Director potentially put them in jeopardy of conflicting statements — a dangerous possibility. Jeff Nielsen remembered a reception where Jim Chatenay started speaking to the locals in French, as he was fluent in both French and German. "Jim started talking and laughing with some of the participants in French and the CWB reps got really agitated. They had no idea what he was saying to anyone. The CWB had a lot at stake during these rounds as a State Trading Agency, and they were particularly sensitive to the WBGA's involvement, concerned about what Chatenay might have been representing as a Director of the CWB. We really stirred things up while we were there!"

Most memorable to Nielsen was their first meeting with the Trade Negotiating team. "The first day we went to the Canadian mission to be debriefed on the day's talks by Steve. We got there early, sat in the front row, and when Steve came out, he looked at us and said, 'Who the heck are you?' He was used to large stakeholder groups representing the Supply Management sector. Since we were the first people to attend the sessions who supported free trade and open market access it became a different message from Canada. Many international participants confided with us they were surprised this feeling even existed in Canada at all. Canada was known as a nation opposed to that during these sessions. I think even Steve Verheul was happy to have a different viewpoint to represent. We were really happy for the opportunity to share our views and support reductions in trade barriers. It actually got to the point that Verheul would reach out to make sure we were coming to the next round of talks. When we didn't attend, the supply management groups were quite vocal, but when we were there, they didn't say a word. I went to three WTO negotiations representing WBGA but we had someone there for six sessions in total."

Participation on the global scale of the WTO negotiations was a milestone for the WBGA and other free-trade minded farm groups. From a modest beginning in a Carseland Community Hall to an international panel of trade negotiators in Geneva, Switzerland, the grassroots organization had come a long way. These talks were important. They meant something. But the WBGA representatives never lost sight of their priorities — to represent the best interests of farmers in Western Canada.

Finally, outside Canada's borders and the narrow views of the trade stifling rhetoric of the Canadian Wheat Board, the WBGA was exposed to the power of the global market place. Clearly, the consensus of the international market aligned with the WBGA's views towards tariffs and subsidies. The experience fortified the WBGA's resolve to work towards ending the monopoly of the CWB as one of those distortions but, more importantly to them, a barrier to marketing freedom.

Doug Campbell attended every round of the trade negotiations on behalf of the WBGA and made sure the Western Canadian farmers were there too. "They were so important in presenting a more balanced view of Canadian agriculture on the international stage and made a positive impact in discussions. Their voice was critical. It was also the largest contingent of farmers Canada ever sent to WTO talks," recalls Campbell. "We had to do something to offset the messaging of the Canadian Federation of Agriculture and the supply management sectors."

"And it worked, or at least we thought so!" says Campbell. "The Western Canadian farmers pulled it off and we really thought we had a deal, a global agreement on trade. But in the end, the talks failed when the United States could not come to terms with Europe and China and that basically ended the WTO round without an agreement. We were so close, but last minute actions were the downfall of the whole agreement. It was very disappointing."

Doug McBain did return to Canada with something useful, a juicy tidbit of information to share with Western Canadian farmers. In testimony provided by the Canadian Wheat Board to the WTO they made a statement, but in Canada's federal court they made another statement which completely contradicted their claim to the WTO. In all future papers and WBGA publications Doug authored for the next year or so he ended his piece by quoting that contradiction.

To the WTO the CWB claimed "it was in essence a farmer co-operative...subject to no direction, supervision or influence by the Government of Canada.

In the Federal Court of Canada the CWB states "the Board was not and is not accountable to individual producers. Rather, the Board is accountable only to parliament. Therefore, neither the Board or the Crown owed any legal duty to the plaintiffs (Farmers).

This incongruent pair of quotes from the CWB became an enormous embarrassment for them every time Doug signed off on an editorial or public announcement.

Grain Vision (2005)

The power of the CWB grew year over year and decade over decade as they gradually inserted the organization in all aspects of the grain industry. From transportation rates and car allocations to elevation tariffs and commodity grading, the CWB held the final and, most often, the only word. To oppose the CWB generally meant some form of penalty in the form of fewer car allocations, reduced use of export terminals or exclusion from export deals. Grain, chemical and fertilizer companies all tip-toed around the CWB preferring not to anger it and cause a negative affect to their revenues.

In spite of trying to go with the flow and accept the status quo, these same companies didn't like the larger trends the industry was experiencing. Businesses were not thriving and the Canadian agriculture economy was not growing at the same rate as other countries around the world. Corporate investments were not meeting shareholder expectations and neither they nor their farmer customers were experiencing the level of success they should be. The market place wasn't working as well as it could and should.

The problems expressed themselves in several ways. Commodity prices languished and exports were unremarkable. Margins were thin and a Western Canadian drought in 2002 added to the financial malaise. Across the entire value chain, apprehension spread regarding declining Canadian market shares, an absence of new investment creating value-added revenues made worse by a concerning void of effective federal government leadership, especially in the agricultural sector. For grain producers, processors, crop input companies, grain handlers and exporters the problem was becoming urgent. A new plan was required, a plan that was innovative, proactive and market driven. A plan that didn't include the Canadian Wheat Board.

In preparation for the WTO meetings in Geneva, Nithi Govindasamy, now a Deputy Minister for Agriculture based in Regina, hosted a private, "invitation only" meeting with the leaders from the commodity groups. "We invited quite a few people' and, to our surprise, everyone showed up," says Govindasamy. "That spoke volumes to the widespread concerns across the entire ag sector in Western Canada. The CWB was insidious, with control over price, transportation, ports and even company margins. They were inhibiting growth and prosperity across the value chain," he stated.

The secretive group formalized under the name "Grain Vision" bringing together a diverse consortium of participants from Western Canadian agriculture. They elected Paul Orsak, a Binscarth, Manitoba farmer and veteran of the Western Canadian Wheat Growers as chairman. Paul Earl, a former UUG employee and WCWGA representative helped develop Grain Vision alongside Orsak. The group's meetings were fairly clandestine at first due to the sensitive nature of their discussions — primarily the removal of the CWB. "That was our main focus," recalls Govindasamy. "Everyone in attendance had a lot at stake. All agreed, the CWB had to go if the industry was to survive." They hoped that by speaking up as an anonymous collective, the government would be forced to act.

Take-aways from the international DOHA Round at the WTO were clear: trade distorting practices and subsidies and tariffs must be removed. A new structure was required in Canada and that new structure did not include a Canadian Wheat Board. It was a dinosaur and a barrier to the growth of production, processing and export in Western Canada.

The invitation to the WBGA to participate in the Grain Vision initiative was a further demonstration of their role as representatives of a progressive, grassroots organization sharing an important voice. Other farmer based groups such as commodity commissions and associations, the Grain Growers of Canada, Western Canadian Wheat Growers Association and farmer owned inland terminals were also included in Grain Vision. Importantly, the WBGA had a seat at the table and continued to be a leader in developing a new farm economy. Now they had powerful allies, all with a common goal.

"People started to realize the grain industry was in trouble," recalls Brian Otto. "The industry was in a bad place and barley was suffering a great deal, maybe more than most grains. Prices were low, exports were declining, trade had stalled and that all meant low delivery opportunities for producers. It wasn't sustainable for farmers, grain companies, processors or exporters. Somebody had to speak for barley!"

On March 28, 2005, Paul Orsak, acting as chairman for Grain Vision, reached out to the Honourable Reg Alcock, the President of the Treasury Board and Minister Responsible for the Canadian Wheat Board with a request to meet and discuss matters of concern to this new association. The letter was copied to numerous Liberal politicians including Prime Minister Paul Martin, Deputy Ministers and all Provincial Premiers. In that letter he laid out the association's concerns and motivation along with a clear statement of their vision.

The federal government has acknowledged that global agriculture has experienced a radical transformation in recent years combined with a long-term decline in commodity prices. The grain industry, in partnership with government, must engage in serious discussions on the barriers to innovation and growth, and begin to develop a transition plan for moving away from the present inadequate status quo.

The CWB has recognized that changes are coming and has begun an internal restructuring review. Grain Vision maintains that it is essential that everyone with a stake in the industry participate in restructuring decisions in the industry. A fundamental in-depth review of the grain marketing system in Western Canada needs to occur and cannot only include, or be led by, the CWB. We cannot support closed-door, internal, and unilateral CWB reforms that do not consider the needs and views of the entire industry.

The message was consistent with WBGA messaging. The future of grain production and processing in Canada must not rest solely with the Canadian Wheat Board. Serious modifications were required and this group had a plan. But government representatives were unwilling to meet with this informal yet powerful alliance of representatives from the west. Grain Vision's primary motivation was not a topic government wanted to discuss. The message fell on deaf ears and no further progress was made with the Liberal government. But momentum was building and the WBGA could see their efforts were paying off.

What a difference a year makes. Twelve months later (March 1, 2006), a new federal party was in power and new ears (not deaf ones this time) received the same Grain Vision message with a request to meet and discuss their growing concerns for the future of agriculture in Canada. In a letter to the new federal Minister of Agriculture, Chuck Strahl, the membership of Grain Vision expressed their concerns. In this communique they had a single message for the new government. The recent attendance of the WBGA and others at WTO meetings clarified their understanding that the CWB monopoly was being misrepresented during trade negotiations and harming opportunities for trade and tariff reductions. A plea went out to Minister Strahl for a Cabinet review of Canada's negotiating stance at the WTO meetings.

Grain Vision is representative of every aspect of Canada's grain industry. We ask that you begin to provide greater consistency in Canada's negotiating position by allowing our agriculture negotiators to explicitly bring the monopoly powers of exporting state trading enterprises into the discussions. By insisting that this issue is off the table our negotiators are handicapped, unable to successfully negotiate and achieve substantial benefits of a meaningful trade deal. For greater clarity, Grain Vision is recommending that the Government of Canada be prepared to discuss and negotiate the matter of exporting state trading enterprises at the WTO if it becomes evident it would significantly enhance the prospect of meaningful reductions in subsides and tariffs that result in enhanced market access for Canada's agricultural products

The past administration chose to defend the monopoly powers of Canada's exporting state trading enterprise to the detriment of potential gains in market access and subsidy reduction. This is not in the interest of Canadian grains, oilseed, and special crops farmers, is not in the interest of Canadian agriculture as a whole and will not improve the economy of the nation.

Once the Conservatives regained power in parliament in 2006, albeit a minority, the agriculture industry started behaving differently. A restructuring of organizations and a consolidation of commodity groups began to take place, largely at the request of grain companies tired of financially supporting so many small groups. "I think Grain Vision was the precursor to Cereals Canada," Orsak reflected. The formation of Cereals Canada, the Barley Council of Canada and the Grain Growers of Canada brought together numerous regional and segmented groups to form collaborative, unified organizations. Ultimately the role Grain Vision played to trigger change lessened as these new organizations became established. Over time, the group no longer had a reason to meet, but the efforts they made and the results they achieved need to be remembered as well as the fact the WBGA was one of the key players in the brief but vital Grain Vision story.

Marketing Choice Plebiscite (2007)

Democracy is a beautiful thing. Canadians are very fortunate to live in a country that includes the privileges of choice and the opportunity to oppose. One of the basic stipulations that comes along with a democratic society is the simple measure of 50% plus 1. The majority rules. Normally that represents the "one person/one vote" scenario without any bias for economic advantage or power over others. The CWB retained a simple majority of farmer supporters with voting power regardless of the actual size or participation in farming. If farmers had been allowed to vote based on the number of acres they farmed, then Marketing Choice would have been a done deal a long time ago. But that's not how it works. A farmer who plants 100 acres of grain has the same influence as one who farms 10,000 acres.

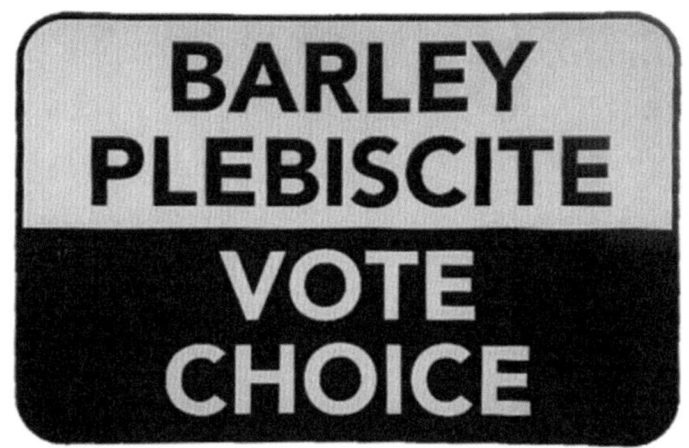

It's incumbent on governments in power to represent the will of the people, whether those people voted for that particular candidate or party or not. Generally parties run on a platform that outlines their plans to run the government and voters give them a yea or nae via their vote in an election. But sometimes issues are close and often divisive. That's when governments utilize referendums (mandatory action) or plebiscites (optional action) for more clarity in public preference on specific issues.

After the failure of the Continental Barley Market's Order in Council in 1993, the Conservatives knew they would require stronger measures to introduce any changes to the Canadian Wheat Board Act. Since they only held a minority government in 2007, they opted to hold a plebiscite to capture the true feelings of farmers with respect to the CWB, thereby fulfilling one of their election promises to farmers. Like any question posed to voters, the formation of the question with multiple choice answers influences the outcome. Agriculture Minister Chuck Strahl made sure the question provided three realistic options for farmer to choose.

On January 16, 2007 the Federal Government announced a barley plebiscite:

> MINISTER STRAHL ANNOUNCES COMMITMENT TO PLEBISCITE ON MARKETING CHOICE FOR BARLEY AND WHEAT OTTAWA, *Ontario, January 16, 2007*
>
> *The Honourable Chuck Strahl, Minister of Agriculture and Agri-Food and Minister for the Canadian Wheat Board, today issued the following statement on Canada's New Government's commitment to provide Western grain farmers with a choice in the way they market their grain.*
>
> *Canada's New Government is committed to providing marketing choice to western grain farmers, while continuing to preserve a strong Canadian Wheat Board as one of those choices.*
>
> *We committed last fall to a plebiscite on barley and last week I announced that the voting period will begin on January 31.*

> *I am announcing today that Canada's New Government will hold a further plebiscite on the marketing of wheat at an appropriate time. Western Canadian farmers have the Government's commitment that no changes will be made in the Canadian Wheat Board's role in the marketing of wheat until after that vote is held.*

The plebiscite was a call to action for the WBGA. In a press release dated March 9, 2007, the WBGA encouraged all barley farmers in Western Canada to cast their ballots.

"The CWB only handles an average of 15% of the barley crop (mostly barley for malt)," says Jeff Nielsen. "Some farm groups, individuals and even a provincial government feel that removing barley from the CWB will mean the end of the world. This plebiscite is on barley not on the future of the CWB. It is essential that barley producers have their voice heard. Barley producers can see the many opportunities out there for them once the CWB's monopoly on barley is removed."

In what has turned out to be a visionary statement, Nielsen predicted, "With choice, barley producers will be able to establish viable contracts with end users such as the Canadian malt industry. This will develop and build strong relations that will be profitable to all parties involved. Our grain handling companies, many Canadian owned and operated, also have long-term marketing relations with foreign countries/buyers and are eager to continue to build on those relationships."

The objective of the farmer plebiscite was to determine if farmers truly wanted more choice in their marketing options for barley. 80,000 ballots were distributed to eligible voters across Western Canada and 29,067 were returned. The results were clear. The majority of farmers opted for more choice in marketing either through complete removal of the single desk CWB or the dual marketing option to use the CWB or not.

Retain single desk	37.8%
CBW loses monopoly, farmers can sell to other buyers	48.4%
No CWB role in marketing barley	13.8%

"We were ecstatic!" recalls Brian Otto. "We had been working toward this goal for 15 years and we finally got support from the feds and the Alberta government and the vote showed a majority wanted Market Choice. Across the prairies 62% voted in favour of change. In Alberta, 79% voted to make change. We were on our way."

Grain companies started booking export deals on the assumption they would be able to secure grain at the start of the new crop year. Malting companies contracted barley directly with farmers in anticipation of a more competitive marketplace. Grain prices, bolstered by the prospects for expanded exports, moved higher. Finally the barley industry had the opportunity to reach its full potential.

And then, on July 31, 2007, just hours before the change was about to take effect, the decision was reversed in the Federal Court of Appeal. The Federal government action had been foiled — again! Lucy yanks away the football one more time.

According to the WBGA President at the time, Jeff Nielsen, "We believed the two strong teams of federal and provincial experts and lawyers led by Agriculture Minister Chuck Strahl would prove that barley had been brought into the CWB Act by Regulation and could therefore be removed by regulation," he says. "Unfortunately Court of Appeals Judge Delores M. Hansen disagreed and reversed the government's plans."

Judge Hansen stated in her July 31 decision, "I conclude that the new Regulation is ultra vires (beyond the power) and of no force and effect."

"So instead, what we saw happen on August 1, 2007," Nielsen continues, "was a dramatic drop in cash markets for barley in the Designated Area. Farmers lost hundreds of millions of dollars in just one day!"

The government's desire to appeal the ruling that ended their plan to remove barley from the jurisdiction of the CWB died on the Order Paper when the September 2008 election was called.

Thirty years in existence and the WBGA keeps on fighting for farmers' rights!

The Conservative Party won the 2008 election albeit with another minority government so the opportunity to reverse the judgement would be a steep hill to climb and the outcome appeared to be irreversible, at least from a legal standpoint. In order to remove any grains from single desk control, it was clear a different tactic would be necessary. An Act of Parliament would be required.

Bill C-18 — Market Freedom for Grain Farmers Act

An Act to reorganize the Canadian Wheat Board and to make consequential and related amendments to certain Acts.

Since 1989, and right up to 2012, various conservative governments had tried (and failed) to modify or remove the Canadian Wheat Board's monopoly powers over wheat and barley marketing for Western Canadian farmers — just as they had done for oats that year. You have to give the conservative politicians credit for persistence to a cause, even though their efforts continuously fell short, generally due to a misinterpretation of parliamentary law and procedure. Eventually it became clear the only way to remove the powers inherent in the Canadian Wheat Board Act was to replace it with a new Act. But you have to be really committed to what you want and it has to be important in order to gain the support necessary to be passed into law after all these reviews. The stages in the legislative process are lengthy and onerous.

Stages in the Legislative Process

In our parliamentary system, a bill must go through several specific stages before it becomes law. The stages for a bill originating in the House of Commons are:

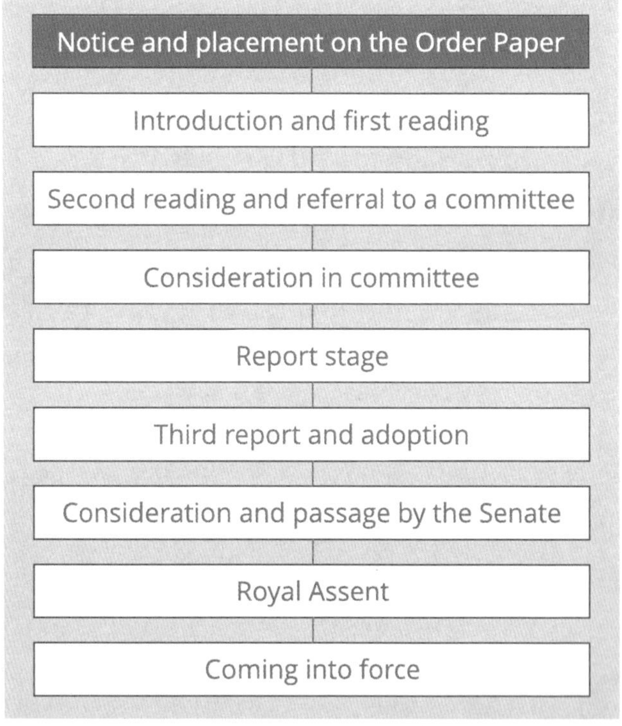

Source: https://www.ourcommons.ca/procedure/our-procedure/LegislativeProcess/c_g_legislativeprocess-e.html

Agriculture Minister Gerry Ritz and MP David Anderson became powerful advocates supporting this change, but it was still very controversial. Even Conservative MP's outside of Western Canada were hesitant to support the bill due to the potential fallout within their own Eastern Canada ridings. That's how strong and effective the lobbying efforts of the Canadian Wheat Board had been. On one occasion, in an attempt to misinform the public and leverage support for their survival, the CWB spent over $2 million on an Eastern Canadian advertising campaign linking the potential termination of the CWB marketing agency as a precursor to losing supply management.

That $2 million came out of the pockets of Western Canadian farmers, just like every other dollar the CWB's Board of Directors and management mismanaged. These were the kinds of things the CWB did on their own, without any farmer approval, the kinds of things that didn't sit well with the WBGA.

Soon after the 2011 federal election, where the Conservative party achieved a majority of seats in parliament, Brian Otto and others met with Minister Ritz in Ottawa. Ritz informed the group the government was proceeding with new legislation aimed at removing the CWB monopoly. "We thought Gerry was just referring to barley, but he told us 'We're going to do it all,' meaning wheat too." Prime Minister Harper's majority government planned on a complete removal of the monopoly with a retention of the CWB as an independent company offering marketing services to farmers. This would include a pooling of profits and any other competitive tools the CWB might offer to farmers.

"We realized pretty quickly that the removal of the monopoly had to include both wheat and barley," stated Agriculture Minister Gerry Ritz. "Ultimately, it was the intransigence of the leaders of the CWB that actually led to their complete demise. If we hadn't included everything they would have just dug in deeper."

A great deal of care and attention was necessary in writing the new Act. There had been so many false starts and disappointments along the way that the government became laser focused on getting it right. The WBGA helped whenever they could to make sure the new law would work for farmers and not leave room for failure, misuse or abuse.

A number of groups opposed to the bill aligned to create a more powerful voice. They included the National Farmers' Union (NFU), the federal New Democratic Party (NDP) and a coalition of pro CWB farmers and advocates who named themselves Friends of the CWB. Together, these supporters argued fervently to retain the single desk monopoly features of the CWB making unsubstantiated claims related to CWB marketing success (supplied by the CWB board). But the facts indicated otherwise. These same supporters choose to ignore the mounting evidence proving CWB management was not forthcoming on the factual information related to their dealings. In fact, in some cases, they tried to hide losses like vessel demurrage in an under-stated sales price with the assistance of export buyers. In the end they couldn't carry the majority or sway enough votes in the house to defeat the bill.

Jeff Nielsen remembers the day Bill C-18 was passed into law. It was November 28, 2011 when the third and final reading was presented to parliament. About 20 Western Canadian farmers were in the observation balcony of the House of Commons to watch the historic event. They were understandably excited and a little too noisy for the liking of the security guards watching over them. The group posed no threat, but there was some extra security posted in the gallery, mostly to remind the group to "keep it down."

"After the bill was voted on and declared law, we all let out a loud cheer. I guess we weren't supposed to do that, but it was unavoidable," Nielsen said. "Minister Ritz rose in the house and introduced us to parliament and stated this bill wouldn't have passed without the efforts of the farmers in the gallery. The members of the house actually stood up and applauded us, so we applauded back to them. Prime Minister Harper gave us 'thumbs up'. That was great! Then we got escorted out because we were "too unruly." We went to a reception area behind the speakers chair after the session ended where many Conservative MPs, including PM Harper and a number of senators met with us to share in the celebration. It was an unforgettable experience, a once in a lifetime opportunity for all of us."

"I was always happy to share a beer with the guys from the WBGA," Minister Ritz recalls. They were such practical, down-home individuals but they never lost sight of the end game. It was very satisfying to see this bill come into being and remove a long standing barrier to the success of the industry. Opening the market created an immediate opportunity for barley farmers to contract long-term deals with malting companies creating a win for both sides of the deals."

Later that year, on December 14, 2011, Minister Ritz rose in the House to make the following statement during Question Period: "Farmers in Western Canada, at the time of royal assent, will be able to start forward contracting their crop. It is their property, and they will be able to move it. We will not allow the leader of the third party[23] and his elves to steal Christmas and that great New Year's present for the farmers of Western Canada."

Market Freedom Day (2012)

August 1, 2012, a partly cloudy, partly sunny day was ideal for an outdoor gathering on a prairie farm in southwest Saskatchewan. For the hundreds of people who arrived from near and far it was likely one of the most important days of their lives. It was Market Freedom Day. For many in the audience, squeezed into a temporary outdoor farm-yard amphitheater complete with folding chairs

[23] *With only 34 seats, the Liberals were the "third party" in government and NDP was the official opposition.*

and a simple podium on a flat-bed trailer acting as a stage, this day was the culmination of a life-long dream. Some in the crowd had even been imprisoned for their actions in support of their beliefs. Their crime — demanding the same rights and freedoms as farmers in Eastern Canada. But this day was about the future. It was the fulfillmen t of decades of lobbying, negotiating and proposing change to the outdated, tyrannical laws that interfered with their ability to enjoy their livelihood. Because today, for the first time in their lives as farmers, they would have the freedom to market their wheat and barley whenever and to whomever they chose. They would be paid full price at delivery and they wouldn't have to pay any fees for someone to manage their affairs. The fulfillment of that dream was intoxicating for some farmers. Grain

companies were ready to purchase their grain; so were malting companies and flour mills. And the livestock business was still a viable alternative for feed quality grain. It was a new day for grain markets in Western Canada.

Thoughts from the longest standing President of the WBGA, Doug Robertson say it all. "Along the way to marketing freedom, there have been casualties. Good men and women burned themselves out fighting for the freedom we now enjoy. Sometimes it takes everything you've got and more. Freedom happened because a lot of farmers and ag industry people dreamed big and worked hard for it day after day, year after year. It happened because some politicians were willing to fight for what was right for farmers and endure the abuse from the misguided, misinformed, and self-interested that sought to prevent any changes to an outdated system. For that we owe the Conservative Party of Canada our great respect and thanks, especially people like Stephen Harper, Gerry Ritz, David Anderson, Randy Hoback, and Chuck Strahl. It is indeed sad that some of our old farmer warriors aren't here in person to share this moment."

"Gerry Ritz was a godsend to western farmers. He got the job done and he had a boss who backed him up," continued Robertson. "Harper understood farmers needed control of their assets. The CWB executives had no skin in the

game at all. They could lull people into thinking they were doing things they were not. They had a socialist mentality that said 'We'll take care of you. Don't worry about it.' What a load of crap! I'll give the CWB credit for one thing — crop diversity. Without them we wouldn't have seen the research and growth in canola and pulses. They forced Canadian farmers to look elsewhere."

Albert Wagner agrees, "In talking to U.S. farmers, they thought we were crazy trying to grow anything but wheat and barley in our northern climate. That's where they made their money. They just didn't understand we had to make other crops work in order to survive."

Prime Minister Harper and several federal MPs mingled with farmers after the formalities. This was an informal crowd and quite a refreshing experience for all to enjoy the moment. But before they did that there was one more formal action executed by the Prime Minister. It had been a well-kept secret that was about to be shared with everyone.

The Pardon

On that sunny day in August on the Walde's Kindersley area farm, the declaration of the end of the CWB monopoly wasn't the only announcement. To the surprise and delight of many, Prime Minister Stephen Harper also announced a federal pardon for the 13 "Farmers for Justice" who were convicted of crimes related to their shipment of grain across the Canada/U.S. border in 1996. Twelve of the 13 convicted individuals were in attendance for the day's celebrations. The news of their pardon had been a closely guarded secret and was very well received by everyone in attendance.

The government action to prepare and deliver pardons directly related to charges stemming from the farmers' actions to oppose the CWB monopoly spoke volumes about how well the government understood the commitment of these farmers and the integrity they displayed. It was another wrong piled on to the injustice of the CWB itself and it needed to be corrected just as much as removing the monopoly. It was a class act by the government, delivered at the right place and the right time. It topped off the perfect day.

"When one door closes, another opens", a seemingly fitting statement for the occasion, dates back to mid 1500 origins and later used in Cervantes 1605 story "Don Quixote", a kindred spirit who fought his own battles against a powerful but illusive foe. A more recent use comes from Canada's own Alexander Graham Bell, although he casts shade on it by adding "but we often look so long and so regretfully upon the closed door that we do not see the one which has opened for us." For those opposed to the end of the CWB monopoly, Bell's version may be appropriate, but those who worked tirelessly for this change celebrated with gusto. "New doors" meant new opportunities, but they also may include new risks and more hard work to achieve success. Nevertheless, that hadn't stopped farmers before. In the moment, all thoughts were positive and new dreams were already starting to form.

Looking Ahead to a Market Without the Canadian Wheat Board

In the days and weeks following the excitement and euphoria of Market Freedom Day and its public celebration, no one knew what to expect. The monopoly had been terminated, but the CWB remained as a marketing agency for Canadian wheat and barley farmers — an optional alternative. Those who attended the formal announcement at Walde's farm, and the vast majority of western barley farmers ultimately affected by the new legislation, weren't overly concerned about the future of the organization they had butted heads with their entire lives. However, they did care about their newfound freedom to market their crops when and where they chose to do so. This change represented a new era for barley farmers with new challenges to address and new freedoms to savour.

Grain companies faced some new challenges as well. The opportunity to purchase wheat and barley in an open market structure required new business systems, expanded financial burdens and an escalated risk portfolio. The expanded risks included hedging requirements for crops that had disconnected futures contracts[24] or, in the case of barley, no futures contracts at all. It meant addressing foreign exchange challenges related to hedging Canadian crops on a U.S. futures market. It also meant engaging new buyers and managing a two-fold increase in their contractual exposures heretofore borne by the CWB. The game just shifted up a notch for all market participants.

The legislative changes introduced by Harper's government represented exactly what the WBGA had been supporting since it's inception — a dual market. With the removal of the monopoly, farmers were free to utilize the price pooling concept and features of the CWB's single desk or, alternatively, sell their wheat or barley to grain companies, dealers or processors of their choosing. This freedom meant more control over the timing of their sales to address individual cash flow needs as well as the opportunity to collect full payment at time of delivery, something that was never possible under the CWB initial and final payment process. It also meant farmers who preferred to deal with a single-desk agent and pool their returns would still be able to do that.

The Marketing Freedom for Farmers Act stipulated a five-year process to transition from the single-desk to a privatized CWB, or its ultimate dissolution. With the help of an external consultant, the CWB management produced six key

Source: National Post — Todd Korol

[24] *Hedging Canadian spring wheat against a US futures contract is not a perfect risk transfer practice.*

business requirements they deemed necessary for on-going operations of the CWB. They were:

1. Government-provided capital (of approximately $225 million) to finance inventories and conduct business operations;
2. Government-guaranteed borrowing and debt-financing for at least five years;
3. A risk reserve (of approximately $200 million) to replace the current government-guaranteed initial payments to producers;
4. Initial government ownership with an exit strategy to enable the government to eventually divest its shares in the new entity;
5. Regulated access to grain-handling facilities; and
6. The regulatory authority for the new marketing entity to direct its grain to the port terminals of its choosing.

In September 2011, the Minister of Agriculture, Gerry Ritz established the Working Group on Marketing Freedom to examine and report back on a transitional plan. Their mandate covered implications on the grain handling and transportation system, on-going market development and research programs, advance payment status and any other issues related to the supply chain. A full report was submitted paving the way for the official August 1, 2012 announcement. And let's not forget those lakers: the CWB had placed a down payment on their order, but the federal government now had to make good on the remaining $280 million still owed against their purchase.

In spite of these supports for the new CWB provided by the federal government the organization faltered. It quickly became apparent that without a country origination system of their own, leaving them reliant on the other grain handling companies, they were at a distinct disadvantage. Similarly an absence of physical assets in port position also made it very difficult for them to compete internationally. The questions on everyone's minds — Were the CWB claims that they could not function in a dual market true, or were they simply out-maneuvered by smarter commodity traders?

The CWB acquired inland terminals and some port assets in an effort to retain a single desk option for those farmers who wanted that option but it wasn't enough. Ultimately the federal government sold 50.2% of the assets of the now privatized organization to a partnership of Bunge Canada and the Saudi trading firm Saudi Agricultural and Livestock Investment Co. (SALIC) for $250 million.

After the deal was announced, Agriculture Minister Gerry Ritz said "The deal for a new CWB ownership structure means the government has 'fully delivered on the commitments we made' when it legislated an end to the Canadian Wheat Board's single marketing desk for Prairie wheat and barley in 2012. CWB," he said, "will finally be off the government's books."

As mentioned earlier, this isn't a story about the CWB so we will leave the full telling of that saga for another time.

Ten years after the end of the CWB monopoly, many industry players look back and wonder why the change took so long. In Tim Harvie's view (former president of the WBGA and chairman of the Alberta Barley Commission), "Grain farming has never been as good as the years since the CWB has been gone! Those who opposed dual markets in favour of the single desk need to admit that and let it go."

Export barley data is one measurement of success in a post CWB market. The following chart tells that story.

It took three years after the end of the CWB monopoly to turn the ship on Canadian barley exports. It took that long to establish export channels, regain trust in Canada as an export supplier and earn markets back or capture new ones. Things could have gone the other way, but frankly, there wasn't much room for things to get worse. The good news was business was improving for farmers in Western Canada and that was the goal from the beginning.

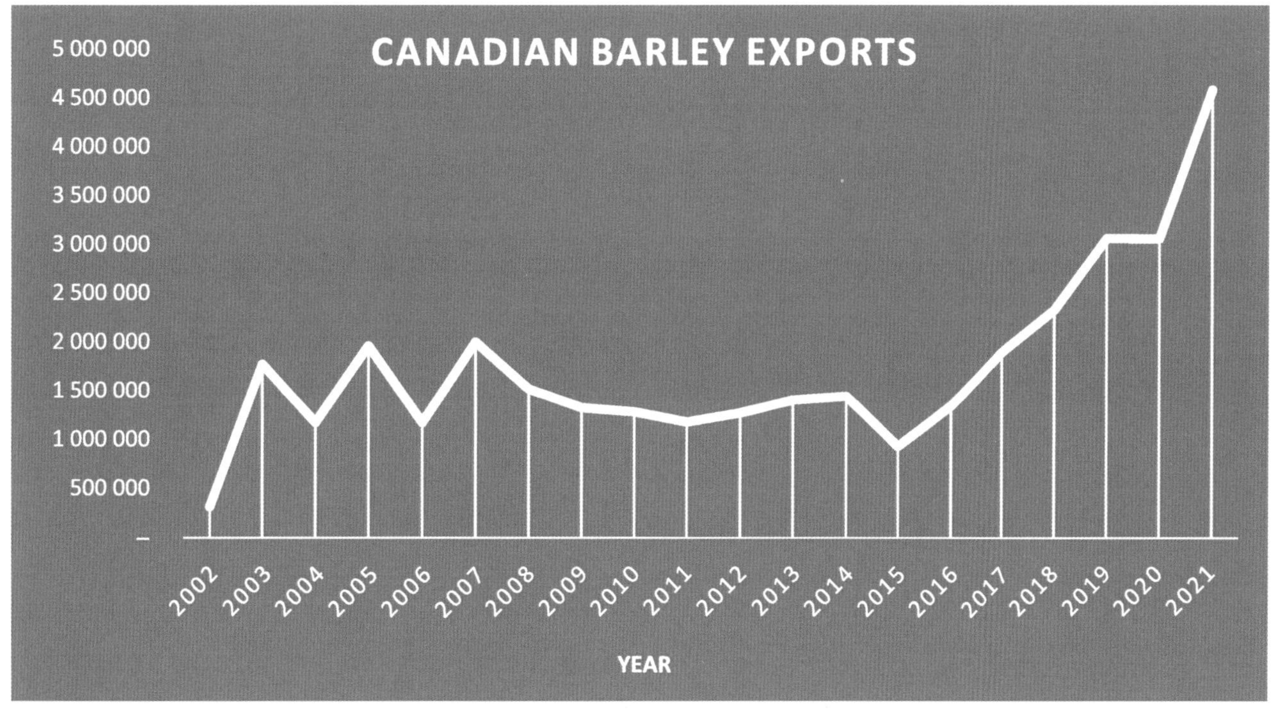

Source: CGC Export Statistics.

WBGA Files

As we look back on the accomplishments of the WBGA it's important to remember Marketing Freedom was not the organization's only battle they fought on behalf of Western Canadian farmers. While it was arguably the most contentious and impactful of the causes they addressed, it would be an omission not to mention some of the other high profile, industry expanding and financially significant undertakings of the WBGA board. No issue was overlooked or ignored if it pertained to the rights and freedoms of farmers and, importantly, to their bottom line.

Here's a list of some of the many topics addressed by the WBGA since they became an organized voice for barley farmers in Western Canada. A more detailed review of the larger files on the agenda will follow but here are some additional ones.

- Plant Breeders Rights
- Submissions to the International Union for the protection of New Varieties (UPOV)
- Domestic Feed Grain Policy
- Grain Handling Tariffs (elevation and storage charges administered by the CGC)
- Western Barley Futures Contract
- Canada Grain Act Review
- Crop Insurance
- GST on the Cash Advance Program
- Western Grain Standards
- Ethanol Opportunities (BBOP Study)
- World Trade Organization (WTO) Presentations

All of these topics—and more—were addressed in the monthly WBGA newsletters, frequent press releases and, of course, at the annual convention. "The WBGA used press releases to make their point," Albert Wagner (past president of the WBGA) stated. "Our end goal was always results, but we took some credit as an organization when we could influence ag policy and provide a positive impact."

The mountain of file boxes in the WBGA storage locker is testimony to the breadth and depth of effort employed by the WBGA boards for important causes over the years. Regardless of who acted as president, vice president or committee chair, the job got done.

Some of the larger programs and initiatives undertaken by the WBGA deserve more than mere mention on a list. They consumed a great deal of resources and volunteer hours by a dedicated board of directors and members. Some resulted in huge payback while others failed to achieve the hoped-for results. What follows is a deeper dive into several of the more complex and critical files that occupied the association over four decades along with a nod to the dedicated individuals who volunteered hundreds of hours of their time and energy in pursuit of improvement.

Marketing

Farmers wear many hats. First and foremost they need to understand the land, how to use it, how to sustain it and how to enrich it. The need to have the knowledge of agronomists, chemists, machinists and mechanics. The need to understand weather and how to produce bountiful, nutritious crops. Is there any time left in a day to understand the complexities of grain marketing? There has to be because it's such a vital link to profitability. A farmer could do everything else right and yet fail miserably because he or she fails to get the marketing part right. For some farmers the obvious solution is to delegate that responsibility to an agency like the CWB. But, for many other farmers, their preference is to succeed or fail by their own efforts. Thanks, but no thanks, to co-operative marketing.

The WBGA understood this mind set. For that reason, the original goals and objectives of the association included the discovery and delivery of more information for farmers, empowering them to make better marketing decisions. Why you might ask, when the CWB was responsible for all marketing of export feed and malt as well as all domestic malt barley sales. Farmers were told by their country representatives and CWB head office management that they were "taking care of them." But, in fact, they weren't. From the outset of the WBGA as an organization in 1977, through the ensuing 20 plus years, the state of the industry experien ced rapid decline by the measures of poor price returns, inadequate cash flow as well as unsatisfactory delivery options reflected in low quotas. The only real remaining market option open to Western Canadian feed grain farmers was the domestic feed trade and it was up to them individually to maximize the returns they could control.

Since the late 1960s, farmers had taken on a more active personal role in grain marketing as they opted in favour of non CWB commodities and away from grains controlled by the CWB. They expanded production, sales and shipment of non-CWB grains like canola, flax, rye and specialty crops. Those cropping alternatives offered better grain shipment and cash flow. The new Domestic Feed Grains Policy, introduced in 1974, created expanded domestic trade and interprovincial movement of grains. For farmers actively marketing non CWB crops, adding this enhancement of trade in feed wheat, oats and barley to their grain marketing responsibilities didn't require new knowledge, yet it was satisfying to secure a bit more control of their businesses.

Of course there were always decisions related to planting alternatives making it important to understand how barley fit into the comparative price options of wheat and oats or the expanding, and often enticing, non-CWB grains. Independent marketing experts began filling this gap in knowledge and marketing techniques helping farmers understand the options and benefits of pre-pricing for deferred delivery or storing grain for later sale. This even included techniques to capture carrying charges available in the market through the use of futures contracts. Some of the more sophisticated farmers opened futures accounts and started hedging (and speculating) with that tool. They began flexing their muscles as they started to understand the nuances of grain marketing, of futures markets and options trading. The WBGA recognized a general knowledge gap in marketing and undertook to provide basic knowledge and tools for farmers to learn more if they chose to expand their understanding of hedging and price risk management.

Trusting the source of marketing advice was critical, and many farmers still harboured a lack of trust toward grain companies. After all, if the grain company was both the buyer and the market advisor it certainly seemed like a conflict of interest. The need for independent market advisory services began to grow and the WBGA took on the responsibility to supply and sustain a reliable flow of market advice. Through their monthly newsletters and annual conventions, the WBGA made market analysis a regular topic.

Initially, Alberta Agriculture employees and market experts like Dwayne Couldwell and Charlie Pearson offered their take on market information, hedging strategies and agricultural report analysis. Later on, newsletter segments were also supplied by Patricia Tuer, a Grain Analyst with Richardson Greenshields, Wayne Steb-

Agricultural Commodity Prices Near Record Levels

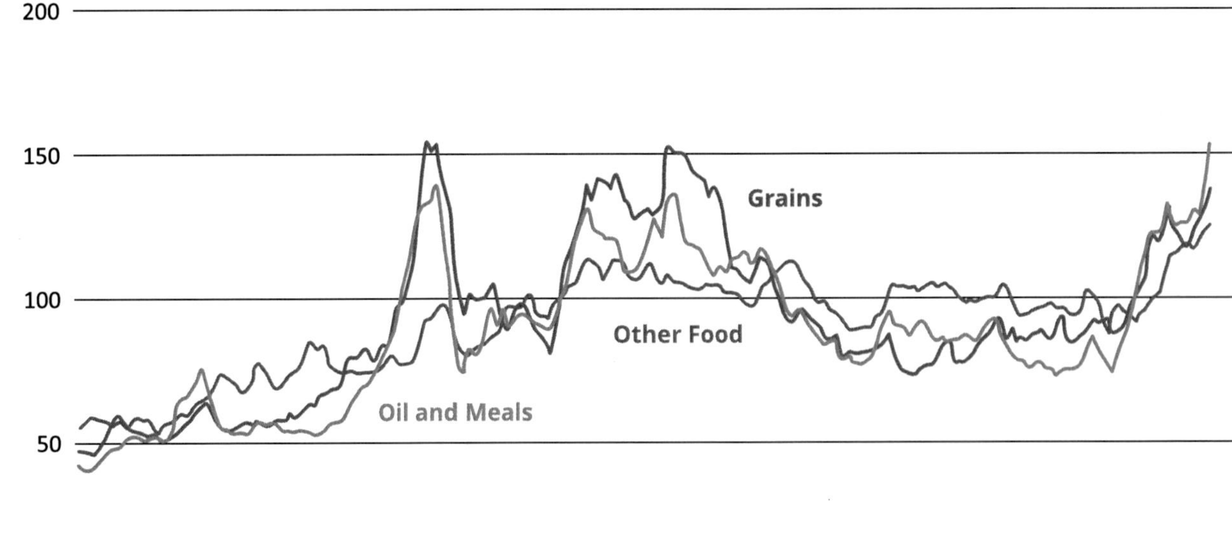

Source: World Bank

be from Midland Walwyn and Liz McCue in the popular "If You Aren't Hedged You're Speculating" series of newsletter articles. The WBGA also hosted barley marketing seminars led by Leroy Louwagie in the mid 1980s and offered market analysis pieces authored by Paul Cassidy of Mitcon Commodities. And let's not forget Tim Ball's interesting take on weather outlooks and what farmers could do to manage those risks.

Barley marketing took a front seat when it came to the mandate of the WBGA over the years. In addition to advice on grain marketing, they worked closely with both the feed and malt industries to engage and inform farmers on the most recent developments. This included the development of new barley futures contracts on the Winnipeg Commodity Exchange (Later ICE Futures Canada), the clearinghouse project, producer cars and fulfilling malting company needs. These initiatives helped fill that large knowledge gap for barley farmers at a critical time in the evolution of the barley industry.

Barley Sector Analysis (2012)

Another example of the WBGA's solution-oriented approach to meaningful discussion toward a better version of the CWB was their investment in developing the business case assessment of the barley sector in March 2012. The overall goal of the Barley Sector Analysis (BSA) project was to discover an optimal marketing structure for Canadian barley. What was the best system to facilitate barley trade for all parties? The intent of the study was to determine how Canada could reverse the trend of lower profits and reduced plantings for barley growers.

This study was commissioned one year earlier and, unaware of the momentous changes about to come in six short months, the WBGA continued to develop this vision for dual markets. Midway through the project the federal government announced its decision to remove the CWB monopoly, so the BSA project adopted a mid project change in scope. Although it was included in the original scope, more attention would be focused on addressing the basic market infrastructure necessary for a successful transition from a monopoly to a dual market. It became critical to identify the main changes coming as a result of barley deregulation and for farmers, industry and government to position the industry for success.

> "An important role the WBGA provided to the grain industry over the years was supporting important studies on many relevant issues from transportation to marketing to education," noted John De Pape, a consultant on the BSA project. "They dug into issues, explained the opportunities or impediments and often provided practical alternatives or new directions to improve the market."

The BSA project used a weighted scoring system for key features of an optimal market and scored seven different marketing systems against the criteria. The dual market option achieved the highest score as it offered the characteristics of an open market with the added benefit of competition from a single-desk marketing option.

ALTERNATIVE	SCORE
Dual Market	317
Open Market	309
Oligopoly	191
Continental Market	172
Open Domestic Market	123
Single Desk	111
Status Quo	107

The comparison concluded:

> *It is clear through this process that the Open Market and the open "Dual" Market are the most optimal of the alternatives. (The open "dual" market is defined as an open market with the added component of a pool offering through an independent party (CWB) although the grain would be handled by conventional grain firms.)*

This analysis was somewhat moot as the project concluded but the remaining deliverables of the Barley Sector Analysis were now extremely relevant.

The report identified the things which would likely evolve independently such as new customers, transportation efficiencies, quality standards, contractual standards and market information services. It also identified things requiring leadership and government action such as industry restructuring, research, price transparency and risk mitigation tools along with enhanced market development.

Numerous recommendations were provided by the report in typical WBGA fashion — one that was solution oriented. No one else was offering any form of proactive assessment to anticipate transitional challenges and develop possible strategies. The grain trade felt no real need to collaborate in a new, competitive market and the CWB had their head in the sand, choosing instead to focus their efforts on reversing the Conservative government's decision. In retrospect the report's conclusions were extremely accurate and some, but not all of its recommendations were undertaken.

Transportation

The cost of moving grain to markets was another segment of the value chain that came out of farmers' pockets. For that reason it was important to understand these costs and to have some influence in determining fair value for those services. But here's the rub — even though farmers foot the bill for the cost to move grain to export markets by way of deductions from their settlement cheques, they had very little knowledge about those costs. Once again, under the CWB managed system, these costs were paid by the CWB and largely unaccountable back to the farmer. The WBGA established a Transportation Committee very early in its formation in order to increase understanding of this cost item as well as attempt to gain a voice on the subject.

During the late 1970s and early 1980s there were some rumblings from both the domestic feed trade and international markets that the legislated (cheap) freight costs to export terminals were becoming an international trade issue as well as a discouragement for domestic feed markets. Low, subsidized export freight rates meant artificially higher prices for the livestock industry. They were also resulting in a disincentive to the railroads as they weren't making any money hauling grain. The topic was beginning to reach a boiling point, but farmers were mostly oblivious to the signals.

To understand the freight cost structure a little better, it's important to know the actual freight invoice for shipments of grain to export terminals or even to local feed markets is initially paid by the buyer — the end user or the grain company — as part of their full cost. Some argue the farmer doesn't pay the freight, the grain companies pay it to the trucker or the railroad. But make no mistake, the person who "pays the freight" is the farmer. The costs, like elevation charges and levies, are all deducted from the cash ticket. The best measure is this — if transportation rates increased, the buyer doesn't pay more — the farmer receives less. That makes it pretty clear doesn't it? Prior to the 1980s, freight increases weren't a consideration due to the fixed rates for export shipment known as the Crow Rate Agreement. But when the federal Liberal government started talking about removing this "perpetual subsidy" it became the farmers' business. And it quickly became another file for the WBGA.

For those less familiar with the history of the Crow Rate Agreement, it's worth taking a step back to its origin and purpose.

The Crow Rate

In 1897, Ottawa signed a deal with CP Rail providing a $3.4 million subsidy to build a rail line from Lethbridge, Alberta, to Nelson, B.C. (through the Crowsnest Pass). In return, the railway agreed to reduced freight rates on eastbound grain and westbound "settlers' effects" in perpetuity. These were known as the Crowsnest Pass Agreement and Rates.

To put it in perspective, the Crow Rate guaranteed a freight charge of roughly $0.15 per bushel — half the cost for mailing a single letter by 1983. The rates were based on a farmer's distance from port, not the real cost of moving the grain. CN Rail signed on to the freight agreement several years later. As time went on, the railways became more and more reluctant to provide service because the actual cost was far in excess of the fixed rate (two times greater by the 1950's, three to four times by the 1970's and six times greater cost over compensation by the 1980's). The more the railroads hauled, the more they lost; hardly an incentive to provide service. Their annual deficits to handle grain generally exceeded $500 million by the 1960s and approaching $650 million by 1980, so their attention to this customer base—bulk agricultural commodities—waned.

The subsidy worked well for provinces in Eastern Canada as they gained access to cheaper Western Canadian feed grains, while the livestock feeding industry in the west remained stagnant. Western feeders were left with the option of shipping finished products at real cost while eastern feeders gained an advantage. The prospects for the livestock industry and value-added processing on the prairies was stymied by the rate structure.

The prairie grain handling system favoured the existence of the Crow Rate as it encouraged export movement, which meant inland and terminal elevations and cleaning revenues — multiple layers of revenue for them, but not necessarily the best deal for farmers.

The railroads disliked the Crow Rate as it was costing them dearly and this resulted in their lack of interest in spending anything on improved services for bulk grain shipments. This situation was not sustainable, so the federal government stepped in with a plan to eliminate the Crow

Rate and replace it with a new Act — the Western Grain Transportation Act — which provided a federal subsidy to cover the losses incurred by the railroads and a plan to transition freight rates to compensatory levels over time.

The man with the plan was Liberal Transportation Minister Jean-Luc Pépin, an unusual ally for the WBGA, but a man recognized for his vision, determination and "ability to tackle the major issues of the day" according to former Prime Minister Jean Chretien. The wheat pools openly opposed Pépin's initiative to remove the Crow Rate but the WBGA took a longer term view on the impact to western farmers. They could envision the proposed loss of a subsidy as a good thing for the prairies in the long run.

Pépin got to know the members of the WBGA, what they stood for and how determined they were in achieving their goals. He didn't agree with everything they proposed, but on the topic of transportation reform they were aligned. Pépin respected their commitment and in an early meeting with the WBGA Board in Lethbridge quipped "You barley growers are so aggressive, you pull the plant out of the ground just to see how the roots are doing!"

Strategically, Minister Pépin chose the 1982 WBGA annual convention in Lethbridge to make the momentous announcement of the end to the Crow Rate. He made an unscheduled appearance at the convention announcing the change to stimulate export performance and encourage

Toronto Public Library Archive

domestic expansion of value-added industries. Direct federal freight subsidies would be paid out to offset the losses incurred by the railroads. What wasn't decided, and would be hotly debated for the next decade, was "who" the subsidy would be paid to — the farmer or the railroad. Like the WBGA, Pépin favoured a payment to producers but that decision wasn't his to make.

The new federal subsidy, the Crow Benefit, had been pegged at $658 million in 1984. The largest portion of that benefit was paid to the railroads. Later estimates of the size of the government subsidy were estimated into the $1.0 to 1.2 billion range. Meanwhile, farmers received a one-time payment of $25 to $30/acre depending on their location to offset the estimated loss in land value as a result of the higher freight costs. This was ironic as the WBGA's longer range outlook projected an increase in land values based on a more efficient system (which was the ultimate reality).

Over the next decade, the subsidy was reduced annually, but the method of payment remained unchanged with the largest portion continuing to flow to the railroads. The WBGA lobbied for payment to the farmer as an economic incentive to diversify the economy and promote value-added expansion on the prairies. The government listened but ignored their proposals and rationale. They chose to align with the prairie pools who claimed to be speaking for the farmers.

Finally, in 1993, the issue of the freight subsidy came to a head for the federal government during negotiations on the North American Free Trade Agreement (NAFTA) and a new General Agreement on Tariffs and Trade (GATT) effective January 1, 1994. The federal freight subsidy was now considered a barrier to trade as a market distorting practice and would have to be removed for this trade agreement to be accepted by all three parties. The whole issue became quite messy.

The WBGA was thankful for the volunteer efforts of many of its members, but some people went beyond the basics to become experts in particular topics. Gordon Reid, president of the WBGA at the time, and Glen Goertzen[25] (Chair of the Transportation committee), took on the transportation file. As the debate over the recipient of the payment carried on, farmers were being informed on the reasoning behind the changes in freight costs and proposed rail line abandonment. Meanwhile, Goertzen gathered all the available information about grain transportation and the relevant regulations and shared that knowledge with all farmers in a clear and logical manner.

"My messaging wasn't always well received," Goertzen remembers. "Some guys thought I was trying to undermine the benefits they had, particularly under the Crow Rate, but I tried to stick to the facts and let them understand all of the costs and factors related to moving grain." Goertzen was vilified in some communities for supporting such a position, but he maintained his resolve and held fast to WBGA messaging because he truly believed it was in the farmers' long-term best interest. He just had to convince others of his opinion and encourage them to understand.

Coffee shop talk across Western Canada often centered on the uncertainties stemming from the possible changes to the Crow Rate and the inevitable impact on the country elevator system. Grain companies and railroads had been talking about "rationalizing the system" at many country meetings. While not clear what that meant exactly, it certainly sounded like it would be to the detriment of farmers, particularly with respect to how far they might have to drive to deliver grain if many of the smaller elevators

[25] *Glen Goertzen's main task as a director of the WBGA was to help farmers understand the impact on the markets of the rate structure and branch line inefficiencies. He set about to help them understand the long-term industry benefit of rationalization, larger, more efficient rail programs and streamlining the entire handling and transportation system.*

were replaced with centralized inland terminals. Some models forecast the number of elevators on the prairies would drop from several thousand to just 350 delivery locations. Without the tax revenue from the local elevator, many small towns would struggle; some would fail.

Goertzen recognized the concerns. "Rural communities were worried about the survival of their local towns. They also feared increased highway traffic would destroy the country road system. They were opposed to change," says Goertzen. "What farmers didn't see was the potential for a more profitable industry for all participants, leading to efficiencies and, ultimately, higher returns to farmers and increased land values. These changes would create a far larger legacy to pass on to their children."

In the February 1987 edition of the WBGA's magazine, The Barley Grower, Goertzen outlined the cost efficiencies of branch line abandonment and centrally located elevators loading 18-car units of a single grain shipped to a single destination. This was a vast improvement in efficiency to the thousands of two to five car sidings spread across the prairies. His calculations projected a systemic saving of $11.65 per tonne of grain shipped.

If the industry was going to advance, all stakeholders needed to be fairly compensated and incentivized to improve service and efficiencies. The horse and buggy infrastructure of the early 1900s needed modernization and that was going to cost money. But it was vital for a country as large as Canada if it was going to remain competitive on a global basis. The WBGA saw this reality and supported the less popular choice of removing subsidies, which were in fact becoming a barrier to growth and diversity.

During the debate, one estimate circulated by the Western Canadian Wheat Growers suggested a 10% savings in railroad efficiency would mean an annual cost reduction of $200 million of the $2 billion estimated freight cost to move Western Canadian grain to export terminals. That was certainly a target worth achieving.

The WBGA continued to fight for the rights of farmers in Western Canada for more than a decade after the Crow was replaced by the Western Grain Transportation Act in 1983. Along with numerous program suggestions, the association continued to lobby for the subsidy payment to go to the farmer. The association was not a harbinger of pending disaster or loss to the farmer. On the contrary, in typical WBGA fashion, they provided well thought out policies and alternatives. Their regular articles provided a deep dive into free market economics and the real impact to the farm community.

The WBGA didn't always succeed in their endeavours. In 1991, Lee Erickson, the current WBGA transportation and handling director, reported on numerous initiatives undertaken by the WBGA on behalf of western farmers — all with little to no progress. They helped formulate a study on the method of payment in conjunction with a federally commissioned group called the Agriculture Diversification Alliance. They sent a submission and met with the National Transportation Agency, and they conducted education sessions for producers on the facts and latest information related to transportation.

Then, in 1994, Darwin Kells and Ted Calkwell, two Saskatchewan-based WBGA members[26], met with Agriculture Minister Ralph Goodale to discuss transportation and the method of payment in response to a series of questions the federal ag ministry had circulated to farm groups. In the end, the number of meetings won out over any substantive change. Farmers never were the recipients of any form of transportation subsidy, but they did become benefactors of a rapid overhaul of the handling and transportation system. Domestic livestock feeding, oilseed processing and value-added industry began to appear in the west, and land values did start to move higher. But the CWB and the wheat pools continued to dominate the sector, empowered by the federal Liberal government. The battles continued for the WBGA, and they continued to act on behalf of open market, freedom-to-choose advocates in spite of periodic set-backs.

Prairie Pools Stance

The prairie pools rallied around a "pay the railroad" philosophy as that stance supported a continuation of export shipments and grain throughput as opposed to an expanding domestic industry. Even though the cooperative, farmer owned wheat pools were established to protect and serve the best interests of farmers, they didn't always act that way. This too was a concern for the WBGA. In a WBGA newsletter Gordon Reid wrote:

> "The POOLS are betraying the farmers of Western Canada by encouraging Ontario and Quebec farm interests to fight the "PAY THE PRODUCER" policy and keep the CROW. The advantages that Eastern farmers have with the present system comes mostly out of the pockets of western farmers."[27]

The newsletter goes on to provide additional thoughts on the disconnect of the wheat pools to the needs of the farmer.

> "The events of the past year have led some Albertans to look at their pool closely, and they don't like what they see. First, once a member,

[26] *Maybe two Saskatchewan farmers could influence the MP from Regina? Not likely.*

[27] *Quote from WBGA member Gordon Reid in the monthly WBGA Newsletter October 1982.*

you can never quit. The pool claims 57,000 members, many of whom haven't farmed for years but are still voting in elections and deciding policy. Some are even dead! Is it any wonder that pool policy no longer reflects the reality faced by young aggressive farmers?

The fight over who gets paid what under Crow hasn't been about what's good for the country, it's about what's good for the pools. Paying the benefit to the railways will hurt livestock and value-added industries, will weaken the economy and will reduce employment forcing our children away from home. But it also means more export business for the pools. The ultimate cost to farmers or taxpayers of shipping 8 to 10 million more tonnes of grain doesn't matter. The loss of economic diversification, society's protection from the roller coaster of a single industry, is of little consequence.

The pools are a bureaucracy run wild."

The subject of transportation remains a hot button for all commodity groups across Canada.

These costs are an important consideration in the calculations of "net returns" to primary producers. The rationalization of the railroads is largely a done deal now and the benefits of centralized terminals, unit trains and "loop tracks" have proven to add efficiencies. An appreciation between farmers and truckers has also developed and both approach negotiations with a mutual respect and understanding of the need to make a profit. Maybe a small thank you is in order to people like Glen Goertzen who persisted in their vision.

Government Safety Net Programs

Whenever you hear the words "safety net" your mind might conjure up an image of a trapeze act with its massive cargo net feature and the dangers associated with the risks of this particular form of entertainment. The fact that farm support programs are collectively described as a safety net brings with it the concomitant view that farming is inherently risky, life threatening even. Well, not risky in terms of human life, but most certainly in terms of the "life" of the farm.

Canadian farmers and others involved in agriculture in this country are familiar with the risks of farming as well as the provision and history of farm safety net programs. They know these programs are designed for differing purposes including disaster mitigation, income stabilization, insurance, advance payments and investment. For the past two decades, the federal and provincial governments have bundled these programs into a comprehensive package called Business Risk Management (BRM) under the revolving five-year funding programs most recently called the Canadian Agricultural Partnership (formerly Growing Forward and now known as the Next Policy Framework for the 2023-2028 cycle). Prior to that there were a number of ad hoc programs targeted specifically to risk related issues. These are multi billion-dollar programs aimed at providing financial security to the volatile, high-risk venture of farming. They're important and necessary. They are also complex.

Most farmers in Canada have tried to understand and participate in the myriad of these farm safety net programs offered to them. They have ranged in complexity and coverage, but one thing is certain: no single program works well for everyone. The fact that these programs evolve over the years in size and application is a good indicator of that. But, like many aspects of farming including agronomy, land management, marketing and financing, just to name a few, the job of understanding the programs and deciding which ones work best (or not at all) is left to the individual farmer.

Enter Ed Armstrong[28], another WBGA champion. "No one knew as much about the nuances of all of the safety net programs as Ed," says Albert Wagner. "We should all be thankful for the work he put in on his own time, and often at his own expense, to learn the details of these various programs and offer his views. What Ed did was to analyze the programs from a farmer's perspective and help the WBGA provide feedback to the government on the real benefits and risks. He wouldn't let us support programs which could be "farmed" by producers, programs that didn't accomplish the goal of a "safety net" in

Ed Armstrong

[28] *Ed Armstrong was a member of the WBGA for over 20 years and chairman of the Government Safety committee for 6 years.*

his view. The WBGA often reported flaws in programs to the government to try and avoid misuse and abuse." Armstrong's focus on safety net programs was preceded by WBGA Director Jack Gorr who, in the early 1980s represented the association on the Canada Grains Council's study of safety net coverage. But it was Ed who dug through the details and took it upon himself to make them better and, at the same time, clearer for farmers to understand.

Ed Armstrong was a Westlock area farmer, but prior to that he was a policeman, crop insurance adjuster and operator of a bulk fuel depot. He had also served as a policy advisor for Alberta Canola Growers, Alberta Pulse Growers, and the WBGA and had an excellent understanding of business accounting. He served on the board of the WBGA for many years, dating back to 1988. His attention to detail and personal drive for fairness were excellent traits to oversee and explain the many facets and features of evolving, complex safety net programs. He focused on the collective needs of the farming community — not what was best for him. He was recognized by the government for his insights on federal agriculture assistance programs, how they were implemented and the benefits and adverse effects they would have on agriculture operations. Armstrong didn't think programs should try to eliminate risk, rather they should address uncontrollable events. He lived by the guiding principle that programs should help farmers in need — a "hand up, not a handout". He was the go-to director when it came to discussing any proposed changes to agriculture aid programs.

Ed Armstrong worked tirelessly on safety net programs on behalf of the WBGA from the mid 1980s right up to his untimely death in February 2006. He was just 60 years old. Ed had earned the nickname "Mr. Safety Net" within the WBGA and his government colleagues, both federally and provincially. He was a true champion for his fellow farmers and had a deep-rooted stubborn streak—a necessity when dealing with government bureaucracy and complex material. But he was dedicated to his beliefs and the farm community is better for his efforts.

In a heartfelt eulogy to Armstrong, Doug Robertson wrote the following in The Barley Grower in February 2007:

"Sitting on a board with Ed could be challenging at times, but I always felt a philosophic kinship with Ed — he stood up for what he thought was right and he fought hard. He never wavered from his principles and was like a bulldog with a bone — he didn't give up until things were put right. Ed was never afraid to ask the tough questions and demand the answers no matter what the consequences. We didn't always agree with him, but he had the annoying habit of generally being right in the end, so it made you examine your own position with a fine tooth comb to be sure you were on the right track. He made us better board members because he was always well prepared and his arguments were well thought out, so you had to work hard to make a counter argument. He garnered respect even from those who didn't agree with him."

NISA/FISP/CFIP/FIDP/GRIP/CAISP
The Alphabet Soup of Safety Net Programs

From the beginning of the Gross Revenue Insurance Plan (GRIP) and Net Income Stabilization Account (NISA) discussions in 1984 and 1991 respectively, the WBGA pushed for risk management mechanisms that would work for farmers, and not become market-distorting subsidies like those in the U.S. and Europe. The Alberta government, along with other provinces, opted out of the federal NISA program, feeling it was too rich and was likely to fail. It launched the Alberta Safety Net Coalition (ASNC), chaired by WBGA director Ed Armstrong, with a mandate to develop criteria for safety nets, crop insurance reform and risk reduction programs that were affordable and effective for farmers, as well as cost efficient for the government.

Through the ASNC, provincial Agriculture Minister Walter Paszkowski supported province wide farmer focus groups in 1994 to gather Alberta farmers' views on safety net programs. Many farmers were pleased and surprised to be consulted on anything. "Even with the best intentions, government employees continually fail to appreciate all of the intricacies and anomalies associated with a farm operation," said Armstrong. He made it his business to help them understand. Paszkowski's farm roots proved very helpful in that process and the input from the focus groups added important farmer perspective.

Two years later, some of Canada's farm safety net programs appeared to run afoul of trade talks at the General Agreement on Tariffs and Trade (GATT). In particular, NISA was not "GATT green". Alberta's Farm Income Stability Program (FISP) on the other hand proceeded, in large part due to contributions by members of the WBGA. Armstrong provided this statement "I personally am very optimistic about the program and am looking forward to the program's first year of operation to see how it addresses the flood issue in the south and the drought issue in northeastern Alberta. The whole process was a vision of one of our past presidents, Richard Nordstrom, and it has shown and proven that a group of farm organizations CAN reach common ground as to purpose, direction and vision, and CAN have a major impact on government policy."

Marketing Freedom was gathering momentum in the early 2000s so the WBGA started to align safety net programs with market access as one of the four pillars of a solid safety net program[29]. Market Freedom became part of the WBGA's dialogue as they linked the need for an open market to the BRM features.

The federal government's new five-year plan, released in 2004 and called the Agricultural Policy

[29] *The other three pillars were Net Income Stabilization Account, Farm Income Disaster Program and Crop Insurance.*

Framework, offered a comprehensive new safety net package. The Canadian Agricultural Income Stabilization Program (CAISP) replaced NISA and CFIP. To say it was more complicated was an understatement thanks to new terms and subjects including "production margins," "reference margins," Olympic Averages" and the addition of supply management products. The initial reaction from the farm community was unenthusiastic but Ed Armstrong did his thing and made a statement to that effect, "We have run our own numbers and found that farmers would be generally better off under the new program. Farmers need to make comparisons for their own operation before condemning CAISP." The Ed Armstrong vote of approval spoke volumes.

One of Armstrong's last reports on the safety net program, before his untimely passing, was a thank you to the Alberta hog and cattle sectors. In his view, the agriculture industry couldn't have made the progress they did on safety net programs without the collaboration and co-operation of the various associations.

The WBGA's consistent oversight and contribution towards a viable and fair safety net program was another important role filled by the association over its many years of existence. The collaboration across different commodity sectors and regions was vital to the development of sustainable, effective programs and the WBGA played an important role in the outcome.

While not technically considered a safety net program, the clearinghouse project, which ran from 2008 to 2010, was another risk management initiative, this one addressing payment and contractual risks as opposed to farming risks. There were no safety net programs in existence to cover the financial risk of the commodity market or contractual counterparty risk created when farmers utilized forward contracts, a risk management process becoming more widely used in grain marketing.

Prior to the introduction of the Domestic Feed Grain Policy the CWB carried all contractual risk including failure of the buyer along with prompt settlement. The farmer was insulated from this risk. But when rules changed, and they were allowed to ship grain interprovincially and contract directly with domestic buyers, that risk transferred to them. However, no program or risk management technique was introduced at that time.

The Canadian Grain Commission (CGC) was, and still is, responsible for producer security as it relates to payment for grain delivered. But the ineffectiveness and inadequate coverage of this program have been causes for concern to the WBGA and farmers across Western Canada for many years. The use of a security bond held by the CGC only offered protection against unpaid receivables on delivered grain, offering no protection for any other contractual exposure. That problem remains to this day.

The WBGA board felt something better was needed. Ed Armstrong and Doug McBain reached out to Sheldon Fulton, the founder of AgriLink, one of the original electronic trading platforms, to learn more about price transparency and contractual risk management. That conversation led to the clearinghouse project.

Clearinghouse Project (2008–2010)

The on-going challenge to keep Safety Net programs viable and current required constant oversight and input from farmers, in particular farm groups like the WBGA. While the programs themselves were developed, managed and, either in whole or in part, funded by the federal and provincial governments, farmers and their associations played important roles in terms of providing feedback on their efficacy and defining needs of future versions of the programs. Beyond the scope of programs covering production insurance, income stability and disaster relief, other concerns such as producer payment and contractual security surfaced.

Under the single-desk marketing structure of the CWB, farmers had no concerns with regard to payment for their deliveries. Payments were guaranteed by the federal government through the CWB. Issues in relation to how much they got paid and when they got paid persisted, but the risk of not getting paid was not a worry. But, as the industry matured and diversified and farmers delivered more and more grain to end markets other than the CWB, the risk of not getting paid due to fraudulent actions by these new buyers increased.

Producer Security had long been overseen by the Canadian Grain Commission and managed through a financial security system requiring buyers to register and post performance bonds as a guarantee of payment for delivered grain. While this system didn't prevent financial failures it was helpful in providing some measure of compensation for business failures.

However, the grain industry had experienced several significant business failures resulting in producer losses in excess of coverage provided by the Canadian Grain Commission's bonding system. In some cases the posted security was inadequate but, for many, the CGC program simply did not cover losses related to things such as undelivered contractual exposure, late claim reporting or futures hedging losses — all components of increasingly complex contracting programs.

This became another topic of interest for the WBGA requiring some investigation into the current program. They investigated alternative solutions which might provide more effective coverage for the risks farmers incurred with respect to the obvious issue of not getting paid for deliveries, but they also recognized new risk stemming from the increasingly popular deferred contracting technique and futures market hedging programs. A review of the Canada Grain Act proposed by the federal government in 2006 opened the door for the WBGA to provide their input on the portion of the Act relating to Producer Security.

The WBGA presented their views of the Canada Grain Act to Compas Inc. as part of the independent assessment commissioned by Agriculture and Wheat Board Minister, Chuck Strahl. The Compas report was assigned to the Standing Committee on Agriculture and Agri-Food in November of 2006 for their review. One of the recommendations from that committee proposed further investigation of the idea:

"The Standing Committee[30] recognizes that modernization of the grain system must be accompanied by an efficient and flexible system of contractual security that will be understood by all participants. Being at the beginning of the system chain, grain producers require protection against potential failures emerging from downstream activities in the grain sector. Therefore:

RECOMMENDATION 11

The Standing Committee recognizes the necessity of contractual security and supports the concept of a clearinghouse, or other models such as the Ontario's Grain Financial Protection Program. However, the Standing Committee believes that such an important risk management tool requires further investigation and therefore recommends that the federal government report back to the Standing Committee, prior to the tabling of a new grain legislation, on the various models that could be implemented for protecting grain farmers."

Two years after the Standing Committee's recommendation, with no direct action coming from the government, the WBGA decided to champion the notion of one particular risk mitigation technique popular in other trading market places — central counterparty clearing of contracts. Agriculture Canada supported their leadership role in pursuing this concept. Working with a team of consultants, the WBGA applied for and received federal funding through Agriculture Canada's Growing Forward program, Private Sector Risk Management Partnerships. With that support, "AgClearing" was launched.

"We started the AgClearing project because our members wanted improved default protection when marketing their barley and other crops," says Doug McBain, a former WBGA president and a grain farmer in Cremona, Alberta.

According to Brian Otto, "No one really understood just how important the clearinghouse project was or how beneficial it would be to Canadian farmers. We needed it for payment security, and we also needed some form of contract

[30] *https://www.ourcommons.ca/Content/Committee/391/AGRI/Reports/RP2564356/agrirp05/agrirp05-e.pdf*

standardization to deal with crop failures or disasters," he says. "Right now, all the grain companies have different policies when the farmer can't deliver grain, and some of them are extremely punitive — way beyond cost recovery[31]."

Just to be clear, this initiative took place in 2006 and was indeed prophetic of future problems.

Initial response to the clearing concept was very positive.

From farmers...

Tom Hewson, vice-president of the WBGA and a grain producer in Longbank, Sask., says using clearing for agricultural commodities would be "a safe, fair and balanced management tool that treats sellers and buyers equally — and would go beyond default protection."

"The whole marketing scene has changed," says Gordon Cresswell, who grows oilseeds, cereals, wheat and pulses near Tisdale, Saskatchewan. "There's a new business pattern to the marketing of crops. Forward contracting is growing and will in my view continue to grow. In that environment, producers will need new marketing security and tools[32]."

"We believe the time is right to introduce clearing," says Albert Wagner, a grain and oilseed producer in Stony Plain, Alta., and a WBGA member.

"From a producer's standpoint [clearing] offers a lot of security," Bruce Delgarno, a grain, pulse and oilseed producer in Newdale, Man., said. "And it should also allow the bank . . . to have a better feel that if I'm going to sell my product, I'm actually going to get paid for it and I [know] what the price is going to be."

From lenders...

"Whenever the client tells us they've got a product they're going to be selling, it makes us feel much more comfortable knowing that that product is going to be sold to a responsible [buyer] who has a financial liability to pay the producer for their product," Brian Little, National Manager of Agriculture and Agribusiness for RBC Royal Bank, explained.

From smaller grain handlers...

"It's an alternative risk management tool," Garth Gish of Prairie West Terminals in Plenty, Sask., says. "With the changes that we believe are coming out of the Canada Grain Act, we think that it's going to be a good alternative going forward for people trading [non-board] grains — from farmers to grain companies — to manage their risk in the transaction. For those that are looking for security, [clearing could be] a much better system and a much fairer system for all concerned."

From domestic buyers...

"Anything that brings the buyers and end users together is definitely a benefit. Any time you have better information on what creates value,

[31] *Unfortunately the crop failures of 2021 resulted in punitive cancellation fees that could have been avoided if the AgClearing proposal had been pursued.*

[32] *The current CGC bonding system offered no protection for financial exposure of open deferred delivery contracts. It still doesn't.*

I think that will add value. I see it as a real win-win for both sides," Henry Van de Velde of Hytek Feeders in La Broquerie, Man., says.

From government...

"One of the real positives is this whole side benefit of having price discovery," Charlie Pearson, a crop market analyst with Alberta Agriculture and Food, says. "That will be a real boost to the industry and allow farmers to make more confident marketing decisions."

Carman Read, the Project Manager for the PSRMP project, recalls the work the association put in when it came to promoting this idea to government.

"What really stood out for me was the desire of the WBGA board to find a market-driven solution to securitize transactions, and clearing was a solution that worked well in futures contracting," he says. "The federal Conservative government of the day was looking to the grains industry and producers to find Private Sector Risk Management Partnerships and the concept of clearing fit well with that goal."

After extensive meetings with the grain industry and numerous farmer focus groups, the project identified exceptional and unique benefits of a clearinghouse over other security mechanisms such as insurance, a dedicated fund or bonding. However, one hurdle remained.

Russ Crawford, one of the consultants working on the two-year project remembers the farmer focus groups.

"We worked with Street Smart Strategic Planning, real professionals in the art of hosting these open-ended sessions gathering farmer response. We met with 70 producers at 10 country sessions. After a brief explanation of the concept of a clearinghouse, central counterparty risk management and the broader coverage of clearing, the farmers understood and endorsed the concept.

Where we encountered resistance was when we met with the large grain companies. They viewed this securitization as an undesired leveling of the playing field and an opening for smaller grain dealers. They also understood clearing would provide better market price transparency, another advantage they would lose in a more visible market. One grain company senior manager went so far as to express his view, that in the case of market transparency, "We prefer market opacity". Without the involvement and support of the major grain companies the whole concept was doomed."

Senior management at the Grain Commission never really grasped the full potential of clearing either and quickly bailed on pursuing the idea, blaming "complexity and high cost" as reasons for excluding clearing as an option." Neither of those concerns are valid, as clearing is a proven risk management technique used daily in global financial, energy and commodity markets to settle billions of dollars of transactions without any failures.

Without participation from the major grain companies or a proactive position from the CGC, the WBGA was unable to find an entity willing to invest in hosting the clearinghouse. Established companies like ICE Futures Canada and the Natural Gas Exchange understood well enough that success of clearing cash market agricultural trades required full market participation or some for of government mandate in order to gain user acceptance and participation.

Unfortunately for farmers, the clearinghouse concept never went beyond the probative work conducted by the WBGA. The real value of the CGC's Producer Security program remains debatable and was reassessed recently as part of the 2021 review of the Canada Grain Act. No meaningful changes resulted from that or previous reviews. The current high cost, minimal coverage program remains in place. It's some coverage, but it could be so much better.

The crop failures and concomitant spike in futures and cash grain prices in 2021 provided a perfect storm for contract failures and large cancellation fees levied by grain buyers. The absence of standardized contracts and failure terms and no performance security system in place (such as clearing and margin posting) resulted in widespread losses to producers and renewed demand for a better system. An active clearinghouse would have provided a large degree of problem mitigation. The WBGA vision a dozen years earlier had been correct, but the grain industry as a whole failed to recognize it at the time.

Research

The most significant and progressive advances in cereal grain production are derived from research, plant breeding and product development. Plant scientists spend lifetimes testing and working on crops to develop better, stronger, more disease resistant varieties with characteristics and specifications more ideally suited to our climate and in meeting end user requirements. Research time is measured by a calendar, not by a clock, and most often results are discovered under a microscope.

In Canada we are blessed with a number of very productive research farms, university departments, many, many skilled plant scientists and breeders and federal programs that share the vision while supporting the financial needs of approved research studies. But the government doesn't just mail out money for research. The scientists and research teams develop projects and apply for grants. That funding has to be prescreened and ranked according to cost/benefit and urgency. That responsibility resides with the Western Grain Research Fund (WGRF).

The WBGA's efforts to develop a provincial commission and a check-off levy for barley thereby establishing on-going leadership through the Alberta Barley Commission were critical steps towards crop development for both feed and malt varieties. Ultimately, securing a voice at the

Source: WGRF website https://wgrf.ca/research-programming/barley-variety-development/

table of the WGRF was an important advancement for the WBGA and that responsibility was well managed over the years by members Pat McCarthy, Art McElroy and Alanna Hermanson on behalf of barley farmers.

When the concept of a Western Canadian based research agency (officially named the Western Grain Research Foundation) began to develop in 1981, the WBGA became a founding member and a constant force in securing funding and qualified personnel to conduct barley research. Today, the Alberta Barley Commission has taken on the task of allocating producer levy funds to deliver results on barley breeding and varietal development, while the Barley Council of Canada leads the $10.2 million research initiative called the Barley Cluster funded by the Canadian Agricultural Partnership Program (CAP). The WBGA remains a member of WGRF, the agency it helped launch.

"The advent of the WGRF was important," noted plant breeder Brian Rossnagel. "It created an opportunity for specific dollars to flow into real plant research as opposed to previous barley funding that went into researching ways to eliminate the CWB. The WBGA and, later, the Alberta Barley Commission were well intentioned, but their primary focus remained on the removal of the CWB rather than on plant research. The role of WGRF changed that."

Now, a reader warning — a section entitled "Research" has the potential to be a bit of a dry, slow moving segment in a history book. History can be sluggish enough, but throwing "research" on top of that could be a real snoozer. Some might see research as the third leg of the "most boring stool ever" alongside transportation and safety nets. However, in the case of barley in Western

Canada and the role played by the WBGA, the story covers the vital role played by very interesting characters and a take charge association in its quest to improve profits for barley farmers. It may not be edge of the seat drama but it's definitely worth the read — especially the end.

In January 1984, WBGA members Pat McCarthy and Gordon Reid attended the inaugural meeting of the first Western Grain Research Foundation (WGRF) board where Pat was elected as a director. The meeting proceedings identified some major common concerns of the attendees, namely continuing technical research to produce new varieties, improved production methods and control for disease and pest damage.

"I volunteered as an advisor to the WBGA in the early years," says Pat McCarthy. "I had no idea I was jumping into the deep end of volunteer work desperately needed by the WBGA. It was Rick Thiessen who lured me into getting involved with WBGA. My years as a farmer and grain broker helped me understand research was key, so I happily took on the role at WGRF. We rarely got malt grade in the Camrose area, but hopefully, with plant breeding that might change one day. Our objective was to get more targeted funding for barley research."

Brian Rossnagel describes the goals of the plant breeder. "We wanted to allow the farmer to produce more grain with exactly the same input," he says. "That means better performance from the plant in terms of yield, disease resistance, straw strength and end-use quality. Our breeding efficiencies improved over time, especially with the development of plot size farming equipment, but it isn't an overnight business."

The slow progress of research is directly linked to seasonal growing cycles. For that reason the WBGA's Research Committee broadened its scope beyond plant research to include investigation into timely issues such as conducting polls on marketing preference (open, CWB or dual) and яёference, to no one's surprise, the WBGA polls showed a strong preference to a dual market option or any other option which included a reduced role for the CWB in marketing decisions.

On the topic of grain standards, in 1986 the WBGA participated in the WGRF process of renaming barley grades, removing the word "feed" from the grade description and replacing it with a more generic 1 CW or 2 CW reference. This helped remove the confusion occurring when "feed grade" barley was accepted as malt. The malt grades were also renamed to Select and Special Select Western 2-row and 6-row. WBGA contributed to this renaming process on behalf of all barley farmers.

From the outset of the WBGA, its board and members knew research was critical. The concept of, and commitment to, research was one of the foundational components of the association and has continued to remain front and centre in terms of importance for all barley farmers — feed or malt. Research was never as political or contentious as marketing freedom, the prairie pools or transportation, but it was undeniably important for the barley industry to remain current and competitive with other grains and other countries.

The WBGA found that their involvement with the WGRF was perfectly aligned with their own objectives, namely improving returns for farmers. They also felt the CWB wasn't giving barley the same level of attention with respect to funding dollars as it provided for wheat. Decisions regarding barley research being made by the CWB (on behalf of farmers) sent up a red flag for the WBGA. How were those decisions being made and what criteria was considered?

Challenges of optimizing production and quality can be tackled in many different ways. Fractionating and extracting ingredients are two such processing measures applied to barley, along with more traditional techniques of rolling, steeping and milling. The WBGA knew barley had a lot more to offer than just a good feed source for cattle.

But research takes a lot of time and costs a lot of money. It also doesn't happen unless someone champions the cause and invests in the outcomes. Under the oversight of the CWB, barley lacked that leadership. Barley didn't have a champion to ensure necessary funding was dedicated to maintaining its competitive place in crop selection. There was no one discovering and communicating demand for export or domestic malt to the scientific community. "It was a void for a crop that wasn't considered important," says Alanna Hermanson, WBGA's longtime representative on the WGRF. "But barley is the perfect food," she continues.

Hermanson took her role as WBGA's representative to the WGRF very seriously. She recognized the importance of their efforts and the value of the results. In The Barley Grower annual report from 1994, she provided some excellent insight into the objectives and expected results of WGRF supported initiatives:

The ultimate objective of this project is to improve farm income through an enhancement of plant breeding programs in wheat and barley in Western Canada. The improvement in farm income will come about in two ways: 1) By maintaining and improving sales of these grains through development of varieties with specific qualities required by the market place and 2) By improving the field performance of these grains by developing varieties with higher yield potentials, increased resistance to disease and insect pests, earlier maturity and reduced harvest losses.

In pursuit of adequate funding for research, the Western Barley Growers Association found itself in the position of being proactive in its attempts to make sure the Canadian Wheat Board proposal for funding of research is directed by the needs of accountable producers, not by bureaucracies. The Western Barley Growers Association wants to make sure a checkoff is done right the first time and is in the best interests of the producers.

The WGRF achieved notable success in its first decade of operations filling a much-needed void for multiple crops. As an example of the scope and diversity of research products undertaken with respect to barley, the Alberta Barley Commission endorsed a large number of WGRF research projects in the 1993-94 crop year. They included:

1. Studies of feed barley quality
2. Functional prospects of barley beta-glucan concentrate
3. Value added processing of hulless barley for food grade malt
4. Effect of bread products containing barley in the diet of non-insulin dependent diabetics
5. Use of Single Seed Descent (SSD) to enhance the efficiency of the barley breeding programs in Alberta and Saskatchewan
6. Screening barley generation breeding lines for malt barley
7. Screening for disease resistance for future Alberta barley varieties
8. Engineering durable scald resistant barley cultivars for the western prairies
9. Genetic and environmental effects on the feed quality of hulless barley
10. Population biology of barley trips in early season grasses and cereals
11. Zero tillage barley production: Cultivars yield potential

The budget for these studies in 1993 was $356,199. Not very much when split eleven ways.

Finally, in 1999, four new malt barley varieties were registered, all 2-row and two of those were hulless. The annual collection of levy funds for barley reached $625,000. The number of farmers who chose to opt out of the levy increased to 8,900 versus 6,800 the previous year. Many opted out due to low prices, but others didn't even know about the check-off. The WGRF had some work to do to earn more confidence from farmers.

In that same year the WGRF made a commitment to barley breeding research by allocating $625,000 each year for the next five years. Any contribution shortfall year over year would be made up from the WGRF's contingency fund. This was a critical commitment to sustain an important plant breeding initiative.

WBGA's presence at the WGRF's Barley Advisory Committee continued and, in 2001, WBGA's Alanna Hermanson was elected as chair. "Research always interested me," Hermanson recalls. "I enjoyed attending the summer meetings at the research centres and the annual meetings across the prairies. I was on the WGRF panel for 13 years." Alanna was another example of finding the right person among WBGA members to step in and lead an important file with passion and dedication.

Agricultural research had gained a strong national level of support by 2002, illustrated by the annual budget of the research branch of Agriculture and Agri-Food Canada which was now $263.9 million. A portion of these funds flowed to WGRF to support its work. It's challenging to reconcile the return on such a huge investment, particularly as it relates to a single farmer in a small community on the prairies. But a recent study from 2022[32], commissioned by the Saskatchewan Wheat Development Commission, looked back on 27 years of producer-funded research by the WGRF to assess varietal research and development. The study concluded "For every $1 invested by producers' commissions and the WGRF in wheat breeding, they receive $32.6 back, even after the long research lags and the time value of money is accounted for." Barley benefits were not discovered in that study, but the wheat results show a strong return on these invested dollars and barley very likely benefits positively as well. That said, research remained a logical high priority for the WBGA.

"The WGRF provided a lot of benefit to farmers over the years but there were a few disappointments for me along the way," shares Hermanson. "The CWB always made these huge, rosy projections about opportunities in malt barley, but year after year they failed to deliver on them. Another thing that bugged me was when big companies would come in and buy the technology research we had provided and then shelve it. That was usually because the variety would reduce sales of one of their main products. That just wasn't right!"

One last word from Hermanson on barley — "Carnauba!" she blurted out. "Do you know how expensive carnauba wax is? Go buy some Turtle wax and see." One plant science study on a waxy forage barley was yielding some promising results indicating another non-food application for barley. "You can walk through the plots of that variety — it would shine your shoes! And that's just the plants!" she concluded. Ah, the miracle of research.

Feed Barley

In most years, more than 50% of the barley produced in Western Canada is consumed by the domestic feed market. That includes farm fed, feed lots and feed processing mills. This large, vital market for barley growers was largely ignored by the CWB. For their part, more effort was spent on creating a marketing, handling and transportation system that encouraged the shipment of primarily malt barley and some feed grade for export or to Eastern Canada for processing. Very little time, effort or funding went into developing feed barley varieties in terms of offering better characteristics for feed barley — higher yields, test weight, protein, etc. No one from the CWB was assigned to market barley to the domestic feeders. It was a residual market.

[33] *The Benefits and Costs of Producer and Public Investments: Wheat Varietal R&D in Western Canada 1995 to 2020 — Katarzyna Bolek — Callbeck and Richard Gray https://static1.squarespace.com/static/5b12b05dc258b4d03b4a838f/t/62389b38c585b30ea8785a72/1647876924255/Final+Benefits+and+Costs+Wheat+2022.pdf*

The WBGA knew there were greater opportunities to expand the size and economic returns from feed barley, but without participation from the CWB (or the federal government) this potential would never be realized. They shared common goals with the feeding industry and a vision of a larger market offering greater prosperity for both.

It was this reasoning that motivated the WBGA to support an end to the freight subsidy regime of the Crow Rate Benefit. They had confidence its removal would stimulate the local livestock feed market and perhaps attract and revitalize livestock processing on the prairies.

The livestock feeding industry and the WBGA shared a common goal in the development of domestic trade in feed barley, along with a desire to understand how these markets could function for their benefit. Information was scarce, so any-

CANADIAN TOTAL CATTLE AND CALVES JANURY 1

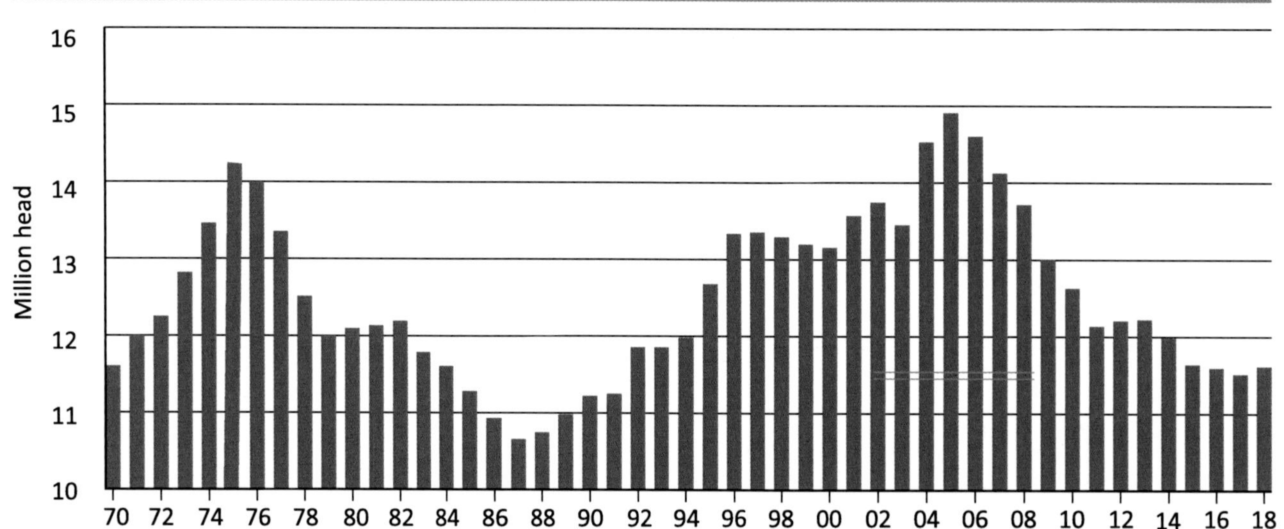

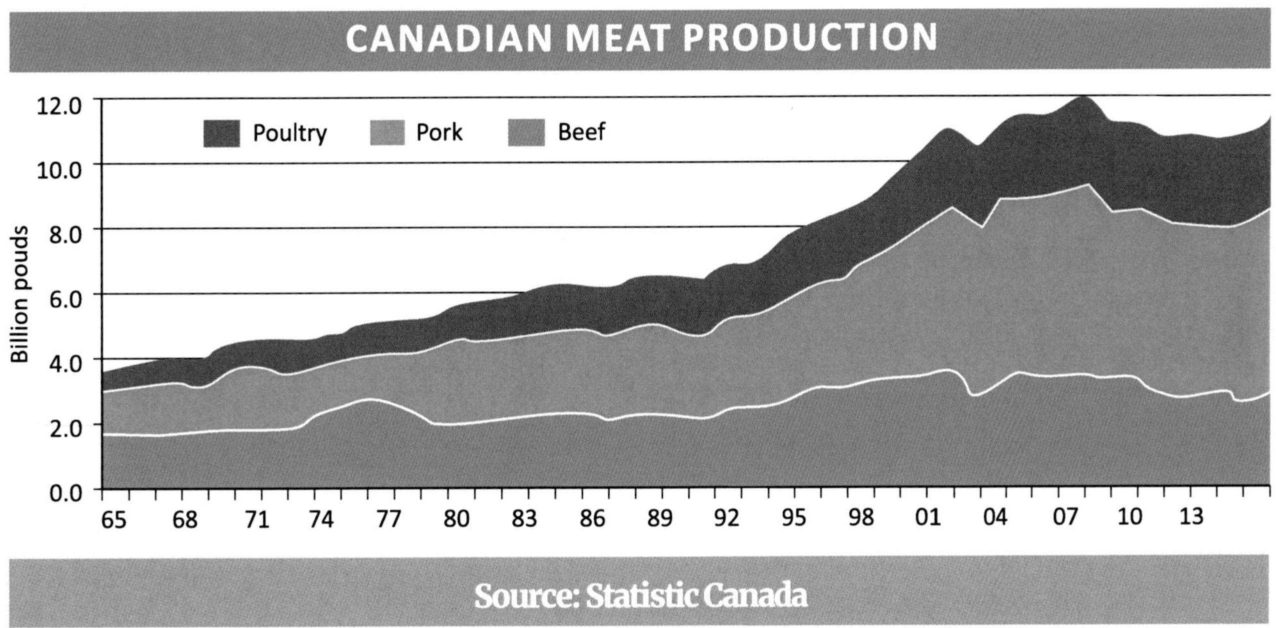

thing the WBGA discovered for farmers was equally beneficial to feeders.

"We started by asking questions," says barley grower, feedlot operator and one of the founders of the WBGA, Rick Thiessen. "The strength of the organization was an advocacy group to go to publicly organized meetings and ask questions (to the CWB) and put them on notice. They didn't like that. But we wanted to learn more about how the markets worked. The WBGA helped farmers and feeders understand how all the pieces and the interrelation of things in the market fit together. The western feed industry grew due to a surplus of feed grains and a surplus of feeder cattle. The farmer needed the feeder and vice versa. Market outlooks and price forecasts were equally beneficial to the livestock industry as well as the farmers."

In 1989 the meat processing industry in Western Canada got an injection of energy when Cargill Inc. announced their plans to build a new, state-of-the-art meat processing plant in High River, Alberta. This plant would augment the existing processing of other companies and reduce the practice of exporting cattle to the United States for processing. Feedlot Alley, a section of roughly 500 square kilometers northwest of Lethbridge well known for its intensive livestock operations, expanded. Some individual businesses grew to feed more than 100,000 head of cattle.

As anticipated, the elimination of the Crow Benefit did, in fact, invigorate animal feeding on the Canadian prairies. Total cattle and calves inventories in Canada expanded through the 80s, 90s an into the new millennium. With more cost efficient production, processing and transportation, the Canadian cattle feeding and meat processing industries grew to fill demand at home and to export channels.

The growth wasn't confined to the cattle sector. Hog and poultry feeding also expanded as demand for meat increased both domestically and for export.

While exports of feed barley declined in the 20 years following the removal of the Crow Rate Benefit, both production and domestic consumption grew. The domestic feeding industry saved the barley crop — or did the barley crop save the feeding industry? Either way, the WBGA played a key role. The vision of the WBGA and the efforts they made in supporting the livestock industry across Canada were critical to the symbiotic relationship and the growth these two sectors achieved.

"The WBGA was a great sounding board for the livestock sector," added Jay Burrows, cattle buyer for Western Feedlot in the 1980s and 1990s. "They were great allies in sharing results from market research through their networking at meetings and newsletters and an excellent forum for info exchange with the feeders."

Over the years, the domestic feed trade benefitted from the efforts of the WBGA to increase market transparency, develop market research initiatives and create a platform for interaction between the supply and demand sides of the domestic feeding industry. In exchange, the feed trade responded with significant investment in this value added sector and a consistent market for the production of feed barley in the west. Feed barley was no longer a disappointing by-product of a failed malt barley crop. It began to thrive on its own as a separate, profitable cropping al-

ternative and rotational choice for western farmers. Western Canada is now recognized as a global leader in the production of high quality beef with shipments to over 60 countries around the world. Feed barley is no longer a residual market.

Malt Barley

Every year, the tantalizing lure of capturing a huge premium for barley production rested with both the farmer's ability as well as luck in securing a malt permit. The difference between the return for malt and selling for feed could be significant. "If you had malt barley it ranked as your number one crop," says Jack Gorr, long-time WBGA member. "But if it was rejected, it quickly dropped down to number five in priority. The influence of the malting industry on the cattle feeder markets made it very difficult for the industry." A poor barley crop meant more supply available for feed, driving the price lower and the spread wider. It was a crap shoot from one year to the next.

Growing barley for the malting industry requires advanced plant genetics, superior farming practices, hard work and more than a little bit of good luck in the form of co-operative weather. But the rewards are worth the effort in terms of expanded market opportunities and a handsome premium for the very best quality. From his days at Palliser Grain, and later at ConAgra Malt, Blair Louden observed "WBGA understood they needed to play a role in developing the malt industry through varietal development."

The Canadian climate and soil types offer some of the most perfect conditions anywhere in the world to produce malting barley. Over the decades Canadian barley farmers established a reputation for producing some of the best malt barley globally. Canada is the second largest exporter of malting barley, shipping to dozens of countries. Canadian barley farmers also support a stable domestic processing industry that produces malt for beer production across Canada, as well as for export.

But the malt industry and malt barley producers had a common problem — the CWB. Farmers were sellers and malting companies were buyers and both felt completely underserved by the

Photo courtesy of Malteurop

government agency. Neither had a choice in who they dealt with due to the Canada Grain Act and the powers it bestowed on the CWB. It made absolute sense for them to collaborate on efforts to remove or reduce the interference of the CWB in their commercial ventures. Easier said than done.

For many years the return per acre for malt barley (if you managed to get it selected) was the best crop available for farmers. Many farmers planted malt varieties and hoped the weather would co-operate and they'd be lucky enough to get a CWB permit from the maltster. But the premium for malt wasn't always what it was portrayed to be.

In one of the many commentaries on the performance of the Canadian Wheat Board, John De Pape[34] provided insight on malt barley premium claims.

#5 Does the CWB Get Premiums in Barley? (Oct 5, 2010)

They say they do. They have studies that say they do. The one they refer to the most was done in 2005 by Drs. Schmitz, Schmitz and Gray (I'll call them SSG).

SSG says the CWB gets more from malt barley sales than a "multiple-seller" market environment would. They say that between 1995-96 and 2003-04, the CWB earned an average "additional earning" of $35.25/t on 6-row malt barley and $40.29/t on 2-row malt barley. Dr. Richard Gray (the "G" in SSG) told me that the study showed that the CWB gets no premiums for feed barley. According to Dr. Gray, these additional earnings on malt barley are part of the malt premium over feed barley. SSG says that without the CWB, these "additional earnings" — the malt premium — will disappear.

SSG took a theoretical, econometric approach to this problem. I took a simpler approach. I compared the pool returns in each of the years they studied and compared them to the average domestic feed barley price in central Saskatchewan (around Saskatoon), which is about as close as you can get to the lowest priced feed barley in the country. If the CWB prices are going to shine, this is where they will shine.

The CWB's 2-row malt barley price averaged only $7.38/t over feed and the 6-row malt barley price averaged $6.98/t under (yes — UNDER) the lowest priced feed barley in the country.

This data shows that the CWB "malt premium" over feed is the smallest malt premium of any major barley producing region in the world.

If, as SSG says, the malt barley price would drop $35 to $40/t without the CWB, this means that, without the CWB, the malt barley price in Western Canada would be lower than the feed barley price.

That doesn't happen anywhere else in the world; why would it happen here?

---

[34] *CWB Monitor #5 "Does the CWB Get Premiums in Barley?" October 2010.*

When a study using a sophisticated economical model says one thing (such as big premiums) and a simple look at real prices says another (such as no premiums) which should we believe?

We also need to ask the farmer — elected CWB directors — what are they doing to improve the malt premium over feed?

The intent of including this insightful, basic analysis isn't to bash the CWB one more time. The point is, farmers weren't getting the premiums they thought they were, or as much as they might have on their own. While claiming to capture market premiums, the facts were the marketing efforts of the CWB were substandard at best. It was this under performance that irked the members of the WBGA. It was a clear example of another lost opportunity to achieve better than "average".

If wheat growers think they have a complaint about their share of the consumers' bread dollar, try this one. One bushel of barley makes 40 cases of beer. The barley grower's share is about one cent a bottle or twelve cents out of a $10 case of beer! (From the mid April 1985 edition of The Western Barley Grower. One has to wonder if that ratio of the value of barley in a case of beer is similar today, over 35 years later.)

Direct delivery of malt barley to maltsters was a marketing goal for the WBGA. Why couldn't a farmer contract directly with a malting company and work with them on quality management, scheduling and pricing in a private deal — just like feed barley to a feed mill or feedlot? Similarly, from the barley processors perspective, why couldn't they secure large volumes of high-quality malt barley from selected farmers who could produce what they needed rather than be limited to 90 tonnes per permit book? It was frustrating and it was aggravating for both sides.

One area the two couldn't agree on was the opening of the Continental Barley Market. While the short-lived market created opportunities for farmers, it did not sit well with the malt houses. Neither the Continental Market nor dual marketing options provided maltsters with the opportunity to export processed malt without contracting with the CWB. So, for them, it was a potential drain on quality grain with no upside for them. But once that brief window of trade was closed, they found themselves wholly aligned once more.

From the mid 1980s right up to Market Freedom Day and beyond, there was no greater friend to the malt barley producer than malt selector, Bob Sutton. His career was primarily focused on malt barley selection through his work at Cargill, Canada Malt in Calgary and Rahr Malting in Alix, Alberta. "Barley Bob's" singular focus was to build direct relationships with individual farmers despite the requirement to deal through the

CWB. "The WBGA took the lead on presentations and initiatives," recalled Sutton. "Building a coalition with a strong-willed group demanding independence was an easy choice. They wanted to be able to make their own marketing decisions, even the right to fail!"

"We worked with Palliser Grain to create a direct farm to malt house supply chain," continues Sutton. "It was like producer cars for malt barley, but Palliser had to be an agent of the CWB to make it work. It took time, but we finally got that working. It was a start."

"Canada already had enough natural barriers to export malt and malt barley," says Sutton. "We have brutal winters, huge mountains, only two rail lines and port limitations. Adding CWB bureaucratic barriers on top of that just didn't make sense."

"Looking back," Sutton concludes. "No one refers to the time of the CWB monopoly as "the good old days." That says all you need to know about how farmers feel today compared to the CWB era."

If you grew malt barley varieties in Western Canada from the 1980's to the present day, you knew Bob Sutton. Never one to turn down the offer of a tall, cool glass of beer, Bob still enjoys the odd "sampling" in retirement in Red Deer.

Rahr Malting Co.

Rahr Malt, located in Alix, was a close commercial ally and important customer for Alberta barley farmers. Previously known as Westcan Malting the Rahr organization moved into Alberta in 2000 and continued to expand the plant and their business since then. Always a friend to

the farmer and on the same side of the negotiating table with them against the CWB (with the brief exception of the Continental Barley Market period), this producer/processor relationship endured.

Rahr made a serious financial commitment to Alberta's barley industry in 2011 with a $6 million investment. The plant expansion boosted Rahr Malting's storage capacity to 1.2 million bushels of barley, up from 400,000 bushels. This step represented a rare investment in cereal grains processing in Western Canada and a signal to farmers of their belief in the industry and a future without the commercial restrictions created by the CWB.

Brian Otto happily joined Bob Sutton (on the left) and (from right to left) Willie Rahr, President of Rahr Malt, Agriculture Minister Gerry Ritz and MLA Ray Prinz in a ceremonial sod turning event in Alix to celebrate Rahr's plans to build new storage and create greater demand for malt barley.

Art Froehlich, an advisor to Rahr Malt, recalls their struggles in dealing with the CWB. "Whenever we tried to sell export malt barley, we had to buy it from the CWB. You had to tell them who you were selling to and at what price before they would tell you what you had to pay for it." Rahr and the other maltsters felt unappreciated as a customer of the CWB as well. "We bought over 200,000 tonnes of barley from the CWB every year," stated Froehlich." But the only time we saw anyone from there was when they did an audit. Meanwhile the CWB commissioners and marketing team would spend a small fortune taking a contingent of people to Columbia or some other small market where they sold a measly 20,000 tonnes. It was really quite ridiculous."

Bob Sutton, Rahr's malt barley selector, also saw great opportunity in an open market for barley. "The system never incentivized barley farmers to produce anything special other than just a commodity. 'Average' was the best description of the quality of Canada's malt barley exports and that just wasn't cutting it globally. The end of the CWB monopoly meant a complete revision of the farmer/maltster relationship. Once the CWB monopoly ended, Rahr was finally able contract directly with farmers and reward them for producing exactly what brewers wanted. Farmers could

produce "ingredients", not just a commodity. We entered into 3-year deals with farmers offsetting sales to malt clients," says Sutton. "Farmers were finally getting rewarded for their efforts."

Rahr's shiny new storage tanks represented a new paradigm for malt selection and delivery. The company knew they needed to make sure they had enough barley, of the right quality, to serve their regular customer base. The open market enabled them to gain more control over their business, contract with farmers in building long-term relationships and operate in a predictable manner. The value-added component of their business was another benefit to Canada's economy.

The barley industry is indebted to Rahr Malting Co. for their support of Olds College's Brewmaster and Brewery Operations Management Diploma program. "The college graduates are important to the expansion of demand for the barley we grow,"says WBGA member John McBain. "Rahr have really stepped up to add value to the academic portion of this program. They have been great business partners for our industry."

Ed McNally and Big Rock Brewery

One of the great successes in the malting industry is the story of Big Rock Brewery, the realized dream of a member of the Western Barley Growers, Ed McNally. Frustrated with the poor performance of the Canadian Wheat Board regarding barley price and movement and the simultaneous absence of good quality beer, McNally set about to make changes. His dedication to fulfilling his dream and his respect for Canadian farmers resulted in a legendary story in Canadian brewing history.

"If we didn't have the barley growers growing great barley, we wouldn't have great beer. There wouldn't be a Big Rock Brewery without the barley growers," according to Ed McNally's daughter, Shelagh. "My dad grew barley after he retired as a lawyer. He grew beautiful barley, but he was just getting feed price for it. He was tired of the low price, and he decided to sue the Canadian Wheat Board for fair pay for his high-quality barley." Ed won his lawsuit but he wasn't finished. Not by a long shot. There's more to be told of this maverick of industry, but let's go back to his roots...

Source: GrainsWest magazine Winter 2015 Courtesy of Big Rock Brewery

The following is taken from GrainsWest's magazine article on McNally, titled "Renaissance Brewer" in 2015.

Ed's father was born in Ontario and was a gifted surgeon who attained his medical degree at age 20. He served in the First World War, during which he met his love — a Scottish nurse — and took her back to Canada. There, Dr. McNally was dispatched westward by the Canadian government. He was assigned to set up three First Nations' hospitals in Alberta and settled in Lethbridge.

Among Dr. McNally's patients was the well-known Sick family, owners of the Lethbridge Brewing and Malting Company. Founded by German émigré Fritz Sick, the brewery produced a much-loved beer called Alberta's Pride, known as "the beer without peer." During his boyhood years in Lethbridge, Ed became fast friends with Kim Sick, heir apparent to the Sick brewing empire. The two remained lifelong friends, and McNally was distraught when Kim told him of his plans to sell the brewery to Molson in 1958. "Ed was just appalled," said his wife, Linda McNally. "He said, 'You just can't do that, it's awful!"

The sale of the brewery was a major blow to the people of Lethbridge, Linda said, explaining that Ed never forgot the disappointment in the community as Alberta's Pride was taken off the market and replaced with Molson Canadian.

Ed McNally was a lawyer in Alberta for many years, retiring from that profession in the mid-70s to breed exotic cattle on his Okotoks ranch. He served on the board of the WBGA as a director from 1981 to 1984. During one particularly memorable board meeting McNally proclaimed, "You just can't get good beer in this country!" In a place where we are blessed with two of the main ingredients, the best water and best malting barley in the world, this didn't make sense to him. He declared his intention to build a brewery in Alberta that made "good beer". To him, good beer was a staple in good times and bad. People often socialize over a beer, and he felt they deserved better quality beer than they could currently get. "There's always room in the marketplace for quality!"

Shelagh McNally remembers the day her dad made up his mind to build a brewery. "We were on a much-needed family vacation staying at a friend's place in Maui. During one hot day on the beach, dad grabbed one of those mini cans of Budweiser out of the cooler. I remember it was so hot and the can was so cold; there was condensation on it. He tipped it back like one of those beer commercials and took a huge swig. It couldn't have been in his mouth for a half second before he spat it out on the sand and said 'Goddamit, Canadian beer is as bad as this American piss. I'm gonna make good beer!"

Richard Nordstrom, former president of the WBGA, recalls his friendship with McNally. "He was just a real good, hardworking, ordinary guy who genuinely had concern for the farmer," says Nordstrom. "And that was why he was on the WBGA board: to do his best to help with the issue of the Canadian Wheat Board having a monopoly, and the farmer not being able to sell his malt barley directly to a maltster. We laughed at him in 1984 when, at 60 years, old he announced his intention to get into the brewing business and make a good beer. We didn't laugh at him a year later when he opened Big Rock Brewery and provided a new market for our malt barley."

McNally was a trailblazer in the fledgling world of craft breweries. He knew a little bit about true malt beers and the difference those specially selected ingredient beers featured in comparison to the North American versions that used fillers and cheaper ingredients. He was one of the first to introduce custom brands that distinguished themselves from the mega North American brewers. In the early 1980's 97% of Canadian beer was produced by Labatt and Molson. The mid 1980s saw five new micro breweries, including Big Rock, establish a niche for their customized brews. By 2006, the number of small brewers had grown to 88 and that number grew exponentially until 2018 when over 700 micro breweries produced more than 20 million hectoliters. Big Rock brews became a widely popular alternative and paved the way for dozens of micro and nano-breweries to join in the new popularity of alternative beers.

Shelagh McNally worked in the family business at Big Rock. She inherited Ed's innovation and creativity, best exemplified by her "hay bale beer can" idea to celebrate farmers growing Alberta-produced malt barley. "They were very popular with farmers and became a great novelty campaign. They also became a target for graduating seniors to 'liberate from the fields'," she recalls. "But Doug McBain discovered a good smearing of tractor grease generally discouraged those pranks!"

Shelagh recalls McNally's time spent with the WBGA. "They were the most important people to Ed and to Big Rock; they really were. Dad had a fondness for farmers, the hardest working, most generous people on the planet."

Ed McNally was inducted into the Order of Canada in 2005 in recognition of his contribution to Canada. It was a fitting acknowledgment of his dedication to his community, his friends and the industry he loved. Importantly, he was described as "an inspiration to other free-thinking entrepreneurs", an apt description of all members of the WBGA.

Barley Council of Canada

After the CWB monopoly was removed, the barley industry quickly realized it needed a formal, representative voice in the greater arena of Canadian agricultural commodities. The commissions and regional groups like the WBGA represented regions of the country, not the whole nation. They were only authorized to address issues affecting their provincial producers. The brief life of Grain Vision was a good template for a national body representing all aspects of the industry across Canada and across the value chain. The barley industry became motivated to create a new body to represent their interests and continue to support growth and development in the barley sector.

The champion that surfaced to help launch this new national organization was the Alberta Barley Commission. "It was Lisa Skierka, the Executive Director for Alberta Barley, who stepped up to the plate to help fund a national survey of the barley value chain to see if there was support for a national barley council. From that survey we learned there was overwhelming support for the concept. Lisa was instrumental in providing moral and financial support through the commission to help us move forward in the planning of the Barley Council of Canada (BCC). Without ABC and her backing I'm not sure BCC would have been created," recalls Brian Otto.

"We must also give recognition to Chantelle Donahue, Cargill vice-president and Bill Cooper, professor emeritus from the University of Saskatchewan. It was their vision that created the impetus to move forward in forming a National Barley organization. I remember a conference call in 2012, sitting in my tandem during harvest, talking with representatives from the barley value chain to discuss the concept of a National Barley organization and a path forward to create BCC. We all thought with Western Canada moving away from the CWB monopoly, the barley industry needed a national voice to promote barley in Canada. It was during this conference call I agreed to chair a committee with representatives from the

WHEREAS, the Not For Profit Certificate of Incorporation of the

BARLEY COUNCIL OF CANADA

"Dedicated to serving the interests of the entire barley value chain across Canada."

BARLEY COUNCIL of Canada

NOW THEREFORE, I, the undersigned, a Director of the Barley Council of Canada, do hereby sign this certificate evidencing such filing on this day, April 11, 2013.

GARNET BERGE	BRIAN OTTO
JAY BURROWS	TREVOR PETERSEN
NEIL CAMPBELL	BRIAN ROSSNAGEL
DOUG CHORNEY	PATRICK ROWAN
BILL COOPER	WILLIAM VAN TASSEL
CHANTELLE DONAHUE	JANICE TRANBERG
JOHN HOLLIDAY	HENRY VAN DE VELDE

barley value chain to develop a plan to bring all players in the barley industry from across Canada under the umbrella of BCC," says Brian.

These were the very beginning stages that created BCC and, in 2013, the BCC was incorporated. The council now works with its members to ensure the long-term profitability and sustainable growth of the Canadian barley industry. It also serves as a national leader for the barley industry by coordinating all links in the value chain to create a unified voice for barley. The BCC focus areas are:

- Research and innovation,
- Market development,
- Beneficial management practices,
- Market access, and
- Education.

Many of these issues overlap with commission work, so collaboration is key, and the Barley Council is well suited to act as the coordinating body for the barley industry. Its members include:

- Atlantic Grains Council
- Beer Canada
- Brewing and Malting Barley Research Institute
- Grain Farmers of Ontario
- Manitoba Crop Alliance
- Producteurs de Grains du Québec
- SaskBarley Development Commission
- Western Barley Growers Association

The preceeding document includes the signatories to the original Barley Council of Canada.

The WBGA still plays a role in the industry as an active member of the BCC and continues to focus on finding the best value for barley farmers.

Part 3

People, Places and Things

WBGA Conventions

One of the most frequently mentioned and fondly remembered endeavours of the WBGA was their annual convention in February. Almost everyone interviewed for this barley growers' memoire offered a comment on the conventions without any prompting. They were always popular, a must attend on everyone's calendar. As you read this, its very likely your mind is wandering back to the conventions you attended, if you were lucky enough to have been to one or more. Most people attended so many times they've lost count.

The WBGA conventions were remembered for many things — the venues, the programs, the networking and the fun. Host cities like Lethbridge, Canmore, Banff and Calgary provided splendid backdrops and welcomed members and guests as the convention alternated sites.

"One thing I remember," offered Ag Value's Dave Guichon, "was how everyone dropped their corporate logos. We just got together as a group of people with a common interest and a focus on making the barley industry better."

Convention programming was exceptional. The WBGA attracted many federal and provincial politicians over the years as well as corporate leaders from the malt industry, feed manufacturing, grain handling and transportation. Scientists and breeders delved into new technologies and applications for barley as well as varietal updates and other research activities.

The WBGA board was also diligent in making the convention a productive working event as they updated the audience on their progress,

Source: WBGA Archives

Dianne Savage oversaw the convention program, registration and menu every year. The success of the event was due to her dedication to the WBGA.

held their annual meeting and developed resolutions and platforms to guide their activities in the coming year. It was always a unique and wonderful combination of productivity and fun.

The convention was the one place the association could put their efforts on display showing members what they were working on as well as providing updates to everyone on their progress. They were transparent and informative sessions unlike any other conventions at the time. They became fact-based education learning centers for barley growers — from a trusted, credible source.

Charlie Pearson, Alberta Agriculture's Market Analyst who often did double duty as a presenter and audio/video support said it quite well. "Conventions were great! We knew how to work hard, but we knew how to party hard too!"

Faces of the WBGA

1. Alanna Hermanson
2. Alanna Koch
3. Albert Wagner
4. Alvin Hermanson
5. Art Froehlich
6. Art McElroy
7. Art Walde
8. Beef Cattle
9. Bill Cooper
10. Blair Louden
11. Blair Rutter
12. Bob Sutton
13. Brenda Brindle
14. Brian Kriz
15. Brian Otto
16. Brian Rossnagel
17. Buck Spencer
18. Calvin Ausenhus
19. Carman Read
20. Carol Husband
21. Charlie Pearson
22. Chuck Strahl
23. Dave Guichon
24. David Anderson
25. Dianne Savage
26. Don Savage
27. Doug Campbell
28. Doug Robertson
29. Douglas McBain
30. Ed Armstrong
31. Ed McNally
32. Gerry Ritz
33. Glass of beer
34. Glen Goertzen
35. Gordon Reid
36. Greg Rockafellow
37. Head of Barley
38. Henry Vos
39. Ike & Rod Lanier
40. Jay Burrows
41. Jeff Nielsen
42. Jim Chatenay
43. Jim Harriman
44. John Channon
45. John DePape
46. John McBain
47. Lionel Bird
48. Luke Harford
49. Mark Hemmes
50. Martin Hall
51. Mel Stickland
52. Mike Leslie
53. Nithi Govindasamy
54. Omar Broughton
55. Paul Cassidy
56. Paul Orsak
57. Phil de Kemp
58. Randy Hoback
59. Richard Nordstrom
60. Richard Phillips
61. Rick Strankman
62. Rob Davies
63. Robert McCaig
64. Rod Green
65. Russ Crawford
66. Shelagh McNally
67. Shirley McClellan
68. Stan Wiskel
69. Stephen Harper
70. Ted Allen
71. Ted Cawkwell
72. Tim Harvie
73. Tom Hewson
74. Tom Jackson

The Barley Shovel

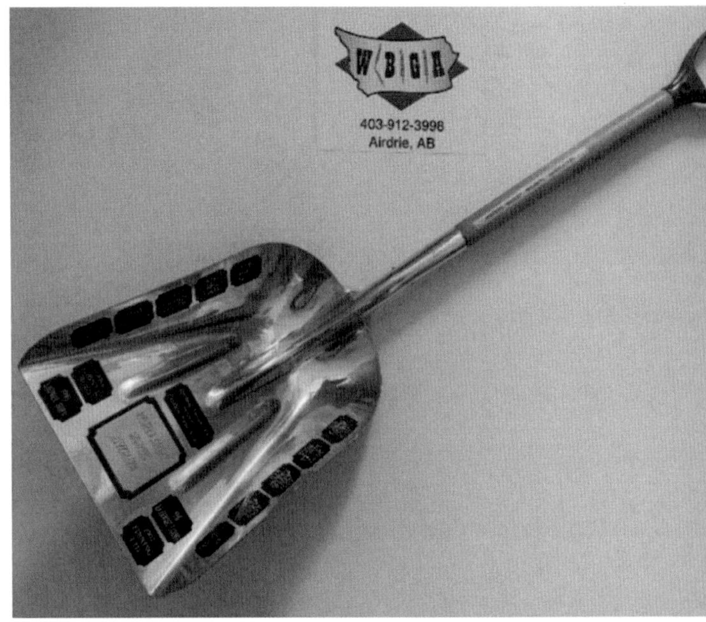

One of the more highly anticipated events during the annual convention was the auction at the end of the banquet. Every year auctioneer Don Savage would entertain the crowd with a robust session celebrating the barley industry and generating important funding for the organization. There were always interesting and often valuable donations from members and sponsors available for successful bidders. But there was one item most coveted and honoured, a tradition during the auction—the WBGA Shovel.

The WBGA was the first commodity group to adopt the ritual of the shovel beginning in 1994 when Alanna and Alvin Hermanson donated it to the WBGA. "Country auctions usually start out with auctioning an anvil or a shovel," says Alanna Hermanson. "It's a way to get things going and everyone in the community wants to have their name on the shovel. It's like the bellwether of a community. So we thought it would be fun to have a WBGA shovel."

The grain shovel was a fitting symbol of the hard work and hands on approach to every challenge the WBGA undertook. It's a grain industry symbol. Sometimes shovels are used in the important work of handling and producing food, and other times they are used to scoop up... well..., you know. From day one, the shovel typified the WBGA in so many ways.

But the auction got off to a rocky start the first time the shovel was on the block. "Lionel Bird, one of the pioneers of the organization, really wanted to buy the shovel, but somebody kept outbidding him. He couldn't see who it was," recalled Hermanson. "He finally relinquished, only to discover later he had been outbid by the local CWB representative. Lionel was furious. He would have run the price up to $10,000 I'm sure, just to make sure the CWB didn't get it." The Canadian Wheat Board was indeed the successful bidder at the premier of the shovel. "I think the CWB gave their agent full authority to buy the shovel just to piss off the WBGA. It certainly got Lionel hot under the

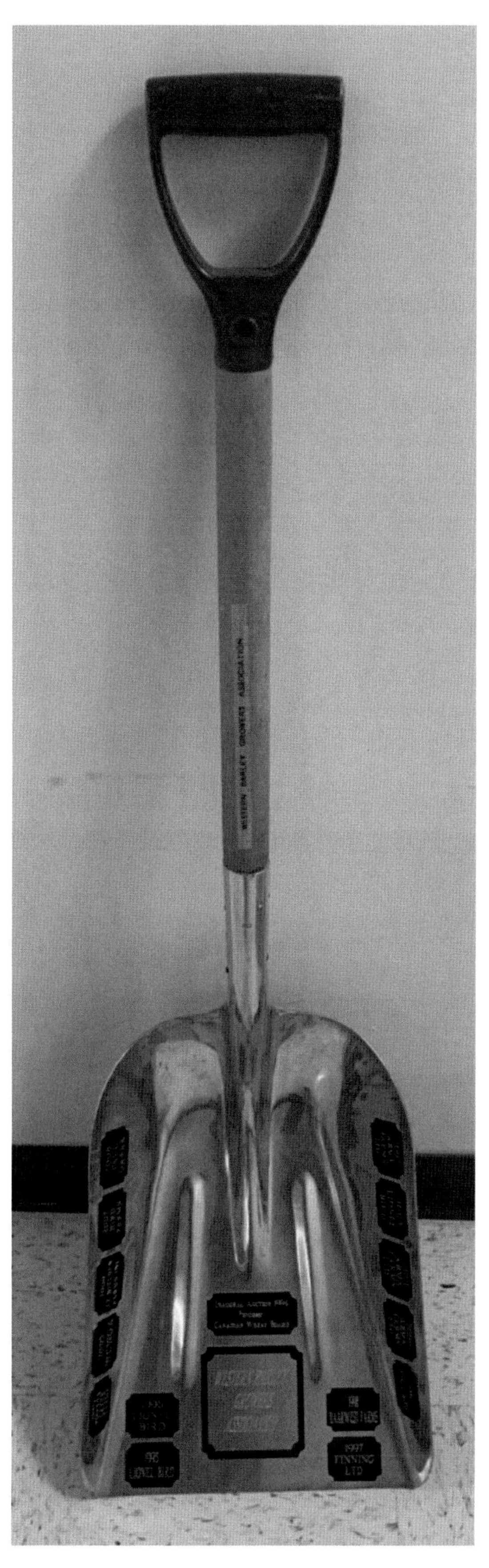

WBGA ANNUAL BARLEY SHOVEL AUCTION	
Year	**Auction Winner**
1994	Donated by Alanna and Alvin Hermanson
1994	CWB
1995	Lionel Bird
1996	Lionel Bird
1997	Finning Ltd.
1998	Haarwest Farms
1999	Lionel Bird
2000	ABMA Farms Ltd.
2001	ABMA Farms Ltd.
2002	Lionel Bird
2003	ABMA Farms Ltd.
2004	Powder Creek Farms
2005	WCWGA
2006	J E Nielsen Farms Inc.
2007	Bird Farms
2008	Paul Orsak
2009	Powder Creek Farms
2010	Gordon Reid
2011	In Memory of Ted Cawkwell
2012	In Memory of Art Walde
2013	Carman Read
2014	Don & Dianne Savage
2015	Tom Hewson
2016	Gerry Ritz
2017	(Not awarded)
2018	Jeff Nielsen & Brian Otto

collar and he vowed the CWB would never get it again — and they didn't," says Hermanson.

Lionel won the bidding the following two years and bought it three other years after that. Over the years, other WBGA supporters stepped forward and won the prestigious piece of hardware, all for the good cause of supporting important WBGA funding needs. Each year another plaque is attached to the shiny blade with the name of the most recent auction winner.

Non serious bidders weren't beyond bidding the price up in an effort to increase revenues to the association — at the risk of getting hung with it if others withdrew. Rick Strankman may have been involved in one or more of these schemes — just saying. It was all in good fun and for a good cause. Several members were repeat buyers, doing their part to sustain the WBGA and support the efforts of the organization. In other years the shovel was purchased in honour of a member who had passed away, as a tribute to them. The shovel served many purposes, all consistent with grassroots farming customs and respect.

Fittingly, the final awarding of the shovel was shared by these two cowboys, a couple of the last remaining WBGA stalwarts, Brian Otto and Jeff Nielsen.

Organization

Organizations aren't successful without the commitment and efforts of people. Elected representatives must understand the organization's core values, the mission and goals agreed upon, and then lead an effective strategy and communication plan to achieve those desired outcomes. It's so much more than establishing a charter and creating a wish list. While its always nice, and sometimes critical, to have a champion, the most effective organizations succeed because they have a great team. In the story of the WBGA, the "team" went well beyond the board of directors and staff. Every member and many industry affiliates embraced the cause in their quest for market freedom and solutions for other important barley industry issues.

Consistently, from both internal and external sources interviewed for the organization's history, the high quality and dedication of the people at the helm of the organization were the main standouts when people were asked to recall what defined the WBGA. From sources in government, to the ag industry, advisors, academia or affiliated associations, everyone attributed the culture and success of the WBGA to the leadership of its directors and staff who dedicated themselves to the goals established in the early days of the association.

There are dozens of stories that recount tales of long hours spent driving, late-night sessions and hard-fought internal debates. When board members represented the WBGA in public sessions or to the media, they spoke calmly, passionately and respectfully, staying above the fray of excessive fanaticism. They spoke with a singular message, never disagreeing with one another once a direction had been set. Their professionalism was sustained year after year, regardless of the speaker.

Literally dozens of different farmers have served in different capacities on the Board of the Western Barley Growers Association over its lifetime. Their participation was entirely voluntary, and they were often out-of-pocket for traveling expenses. They did what they did for the greater good of the barley sector, their fellow farmers and for future generations. The association never enjoyed a huge membership, but that didn't stop them—they knew they were right. Gordon Reid had indeed hit the nail on the head when he stated "the WBGA punched above its weight class."

With the help of the Alberta government's Omar Broughton, John Channon and Doug Campbell at the start, a small group of committed barley farmers had set about to improve Western Canadian agriculture for all farmers. Their focus was one of inclusion, of listening and of acting. They formed a Board with a two-year rotating President to ensure diversity and avoid burn-out. Their committees were on point with current issues and they attracted compatible, dedicated, knowledgeable people to tackle them head on. They reached out to decision makers in corporate and political spheres, and quickly became involved in pertinent committees and organizations across the agricultural sector — all in an effort to learn and to influence.

The WBGA attracted like-minded people looking for change, seeking freedom to operate as independent businessmen and women. The WBGA board recruited members to let their names stand for election in a democratic process. No farmer was denied the opportunity to play a role in the multitude of projects and information collection efforts of the committees. The organization thrived on diversity and the energy of its members.

Directors didn't always agree on everything within the closed doors of the boardroom. Opinions varied and disagreements occurred, but after everyone had their say, they always agreed on a position or approach that best represented the WBGA view. Sometimes, things got a bit heated, but mutual respect trumped all, creating a strong, unified stand and a deep friendship amongst the leaders.

Former WBGA President, Tim Harvie, remembers his first encounter with the organization as he considered getting involved. From the beginning, he was promised he'd get way more out of it than he'd put in. "It was so true," says Harvie. "The people, the ideas shared sitting around a table, a fantastic education and lifelong friends, all really helped my business."

The WBGA was continually presenting the farmer's viewpoint in consultations with both the provincial and federal governments. This meant several thorough presentations were given to parliamentary and senate committees, as well as government and grain industry representatives. "The association is very well respected for its frank and reasoned approach to problems plaguing agriculture, probably because, as farmers ourselves, we appreciate simple and sensible solutions rather than red tape and bureaucratic complexity," says Doug Robertson, long-time member of the WBGA and frequently-occurring name on the list of its executive members.

"Simple and sensible solutions rather than red tape and bureaucratic complexity."

The phrase bears repeating as it's the essence of the organization. Many people who served as directors on the board of the WBGA stressed the importance that no one was there for recognition or credit. No one sought publicity or adulation. They were all there to represent and speak for the farmers of Western Canada. Their primary focus was barley, but many of their efforts affected all farmers and all crops.

Leaders

From 1977 through to present day, the greatest strengths of the WBGA have been the capacity and diversity of the people leading the organization. Their novel approach to rotating presidents every two years has introduced fresh thought and new energy, while maintaining an unwavering eye on the main principles of the organization. If anyone every did a SWOT[35] analysis of the WBGA, the number one strength would very likely be leadership.

Dozens of farmers from the prairies provided input, analysis and negotiation on numerous topics important to their livelihoods. Doug Robertson remembers "The WBGA attracted people who understood certain aspects of agricultural farm programs, better than the so called experts in many cases. Stan Wiskel on the Canada Grain Act, Ed Armstrong on support programs and Martin Hall on CWB contracts. These guys could explain things to WBGA members and they offered ideas for improvements too. No program should be allowed to be "farmed" by producers either." All of these heroes of the WBGA are listed on Appendix 1 at the end of the book, spanning forty-five years of directors and executives who formed the leadership of the organization, the backbone that gained respect in the industry and effected real change.

One WBGA member posted a public comment in Farms.com's Agriville as a pointed tribute to two of the many people who made a difference within the association. In February 2008, Carol Husband, a Saskatchewan farmer wrote the following, sharing her views on the WBGA and its leaders at that time:

"The Western Barley Growers' Association has truly come of age.

If you attended the conference in Calgary, you would understand why I make this comment:

1. WBGA have adopted a global point of view. Their conference was about IDEAS. Not about people. That's grown-up stuff.
2. WBGA provided a forum for researchers to compare their efforts WITHIN THE CONTEXT OF HOW IT WOULD IMPACT ON FARMERS, and then contemplate collaboration! Not smart guys sitting in a lab, in isolation, but sharing with farmers and each other!
3. Making a place at the WBGA table where ALL farmers/participants are comfortable.

[35] *SWOT – Strength/Weakness/Opportunity/Threat analysis matrix often used as a strategic planning business tool.*

Speaker Tim Stonehouse[36] wrote to me and said it well:

"Well, from the beginning at the airport, being met by Doug, all I experienced was of being welcomed and a good feeling. I thank you so much for the invitation and this opportunity to come to Calgary to meet so many friendly, and good people.

4. WBGA have not forgotten their purpose. They are working hard for FARMERS. The clearing house, the barley research, are done to make barley production more profitable for farmers.
5. The Alberta Government has been an ideal climate in which a barley association can grow and thrive. The Alberta Government does not crave to be the star; rather, they trust in their people enough to realize there can be countless stars, as long as they give up the limelight, and let their people bloom.
6. The WBGA has not forgotten their past. Lionel Bird and Gordon Reid were both honored for ploughing those tough outside rows. They honor their pioneer thinkers.

Carol Husband and Tim Stonehouse

So how did this maturity ripen so quickly? Two prime reasons come to mind:

Doug McBain, from Cremona, Alberta has dedicated incalculable time and effort towards maturing the organization into a classy, but comfortable venue. He has worked closely with Government and farm organizations and researchers and farmers, maintaining that McBain harmony within all camps. When Dougie goes Mc'Baining, no one can refuse.

After Jeff Nielsen succeeded Doug as President, he also works tirelessly, thoroughly learning the issues, staying on track. Tough. Driving. Persistent. Who could help but like Nielsen? Between the two of these barley growers, the 2008 WBGA Convention gave up, and yielded to complete success. Between the two of them, agriculture will be forever changed."

Carol's comments are shared by many and are equally appropriate for numerous WBGA leaders. Some have likely been referred to as "a pain in the ass" over the years. They wear that label with pride as it represents a plain truth that they got the job done, they flipped over the apple cart and disrupted the status quo.

[36] *Malt Sales Director Muntons plc, United Kingdom.*

Staff

Dianne Savage

"Dianne was the heart of the WBGA." Those exact words come from Brian Otto, but they could easily have been stated by any of the members or sponsors of the WBGA. For 18 years Dianne Savage served as the Secretary-Manager for the association, managing day-to-day activities, monthly board meetings, the annual convention and shepherd for the standing board of the organization.

"She was the organization's driving force," Otto continued. "Sometimes we (the board members) get wrapped up in our farming operations and we forget we have another job to do. Dianne never let us forget. She worked her heart out on the convention—programs, speakers, sponsorships, you name it. She was a great organizer. The convention was her baby. She also kept her eye on the news and would often call asking "Have you heard this? How are you going to respond?" She was so important to the barley industry."

Dianne was the one constant at the WBGA. She followed in a series of fondly remembered Secretary-Managers who are also listed in the Appendix of this book, but Dianne was by far the longest serving employee. Year after year, board members changed and new people took on executive roles, while Dianne remained as the stable and consistent primary contact for the board, members and industry.

Dianne took the time to get to know people in the industry personally. She had a warm personality and an appreciation for an off colour joke. Her laugh was infectious and genuine, as was her love of family, her husband Don and her grand daughter, whose picture was never far from her desk.

Dianne didn't have a farm background, but she had a way of dealing with farmers and she wasn't shy to express her opinion—usually within the private confines of the WBGA Board. She generally got along with everyone but once in a while someone would get on the wrong side of her and it would go something like this:

"I don't want to deal with (insert name here)! I didn't want to tell him he's an asshole. That's for you guys to do. Here's what he said. (unacceptable comment here). You can phone him up, here's his number. Give him a call. Let me know how it goes...

As you read that you can actually hear her, can't you?

In the years between 2000 and 2018, if you had any contact at all with the WBGA, you most certainly dealt with Dianne. She was 'mother bear' protective of the organization and her Board of Directors. Her dedication to farmers in general, and barley growers specifically, was intense. Her contribution to the WBGA cannot be exaggerated and her early passing in early 2019 was a sad day for all who knew her.

Other staff members of the WBGA proceeding Dianne deserve mentioning here as well as they excelled in their efforts and their dedication to meet the ever changing needs of this farm group.

Kathy Cooper was a soldier in the development of the Alberta Barley Commission and even testified in proceedings on behalf of the WBGA. Like Dianne, she had a "no crap" way of dealing with farmers that was very effective.

Anne Schneider was more formal and professional in her business style but every bit as effective and hard working in her service to the WBGA. She went on from the WBGA to the Alberta Barley Commission continuing to support the barley industry.

Linda Lukenbill blazed the trail for the Secretary Manager position at the WBGA in the early years from 1983 to 1987 and was a great support for new directors unfamiliar with board proceedings.

In the years following Diane Savage's passing, Brittany Walker stepped into a part-time role of managing the day to day and week to week duties of the WBGA. The amount of work has declined since the CWB monopoly was removed, but Brittany has stepped up to fill some big shoes and maintain the communications of the organization. Her efforts have been much appreciated by the WBGA.

The WBGA owes a debt of gratitude to these ladies and others who served the organization over the years.

Friends of the WBGA

Alberta Government

The WBGA was fortunate to have long-standing support from the government of Alberta throughout all of its years of existence. Agriculture ministers and their deputies and many staff members in Edmonton and across the province backed many policies and initiatives generated by the WBGA. In addition to the earlier tributes to Omar Broughton and John Channon, the WBGA would like to pay tribute to government representatives for both their financial and moral support over the years.

Doug Robertson recalls many of the supporters. "We wouldn't have achieved as much as we did without Ag Ministers like Ernie Isley, Ty Lund, Walter Paszkowski, Hugh Horner, Shirley McLellan and Doug Horner. We also owe a lot to senior staff of the government and their consultant advisors, people like Ken Beswick, Brenda Brindle, Doug Campbell and Nithi Govindasamy."

The WBGA is also indebted to many, many other people involved in agriculture who supported the organization's efforts from both a professional and personal perspective. "These people hailed our causes, broke trail for our progress and supported us in an unconditional way as we worked towards our goals," says Doug Robertson. "When we reached out for help or advice, they always answered the call. They put gas in our tank, wind in our sails or any other metaphor one can imagine in support of farmers. We would not have been as successful without these people in our corner."

In no particular order the WBGA wants to acknowledge and thank the following people from the barley industry and organizations who we call friends.

Stephen Harper — Prime Minister of Canada
Ian White — Canadian Wheat Board
Gerry Ritz — Federal Minister of Agriculture
David Anderson — Federal Member of Parliament
Chuck Strahl — Federal Minister of Agriculture
Alanna Koch — Sask Deputy Minister of Agriculture
Nithi Govindasamy — Alberta Agriculture
Bill Cooper — University of Saskatchewan Professor, Farmer and Industry Guru
Ike Lanier — Southern Alberta Farmer
Charlie Pearson — Alberta Agriculture
Jim Pallister — Manitoba Farmer
Charlie Mayer — Federal Minister of Agriculture
Steve Verheul — Chief Agriculture Trade Negotiator
Patrick Rowan — BARI-Canada
Robert Chappell — Canada Malt
Ed McNally — Big Rock Brewery
Shelagh McNally — Big Rock Brewery
Kevin Sich — Rahr Malting Co.
Ted Allen — President United Grain Growers
John DePape — The CWB Monitor
Mark Hemmes — Quorum Corp
Richard Phillips — Former Executive Director Grain Growers of Canada
Carman Read — C&N Partners
Rod Green — Palliser Grain
Ken Stickland — KenAgra
"Barley" Bob Sutton — Malt Selector
Paul Cassidy — Mitcon Commodities
Don Savage — Auctioneer & WBGA Supporter

Western Canadian Wheat Growers Association
Winnipeg Commodity Exchange / ICE Futures Canada

In Memoriam

With an organization spanning 44 years, it's an unavoidable certainty we will lose some of the early champions. The WBGA is indebted to so many people for their contributions, and there's a special place in our hearts for those who are no longer with us to enjoy the successes we achieved together. The WBGA honours those who were members and active participants in the history of the organization. They will forever remain part of our legacy.

Art Mainil
Art Walde
Brian Adam
Cal Ausenhus
Chris Carruthers
Dianne Savage
Ed Armstrong
Eugene Boyko
Gordon Reid
John Channon
Ken Beswick
Leo Meyer Sr.
Lionel Bird
Mike Leslie
Omar Broughton
Stan Wiskel
Ted Cawkwell

Part 4

WBGA Legacy

Many accomplishments were achieved during the years of the WBGA's existence thanks to their own initiatives or in collaboration with others. They include the end of the CWB monopoly, the end of the Crow Rate, transparent markets, improved knowledge on issues such as transportation, safety programs, research and grain marketing — all excellent examples of tangible contributions to the farm community. Many individuals contributed to this body of work, but they didn't seek credit, only results. The legacy of the WBGA is a reflection on those things that survive the people and the organization. Many WBGA participants view their legacy in the context as a gift to their children. They did what they did so those that followed would have a better industry.

A "legacy or heritage" can be defined *as something that someone has achieved that continues to exist after they stop; a gift.*[37] When one looks at the body of achievements of the Western Barley Growers Association, its members, directors and staff since its inception in 1977, many legacies come to mind.

A common view held by many people who provided comments to this retrospective of the WBGA is the sense that the industry owes a debt of gratitude to everyone who helped move these initiatives down the road. The barley industry in Western Canada, and agriculture overall, are better for the existence of the WBGA.

[37] *Macmillan dictionary https://www.macmillandictionary.com/dictionary/british/legacy.*

Some Parting Comments

Many people shared their final thoughts on the legacy of the WBGA and we share them here as a closing tribute:

"The members of the WBGA brought a different outlook to the table. We were "young and cocky" and, in some cases, "young and dumb" but we persevered and learned from our mistakes." — Rick Thiessen.

"Many of the changes in the grain industry are a result of WBGA actions." — Lloyd Groeneveld.

"The WBGA was instrumental in deregulating the CWB. We never wanted the CWB to disappear; we just wanted choice and now we have it." — Buck Spencer.

"Our legacy was our ability to connect and communicate with government leaders so they could hear the story from real farmers. We showed them we were people of character, dedicated and intelligent people who spoke for change." — Richard Nordstrom.

"The WBGA would seek out and develop good ideas to help farmers, and then let them evolve on their own. Our studies helped move things along and helped farmers in the process." — Doug Robertson.

"The WBGA stood for free and open markets and showed the way to work with government, regulators and commercial interests. The WBGA should be remembered as a positive influence in creating solutions benefiting all farmers. Agriculture in Western Canada is better off due to the WBGA. The economy is better off due to them as well." — Albert Wagner.

"The WBGA should be remembered as a strong voice for farmers focused on finding better feed and malt markets for barley farmers. The work accomplished on market development, value added and important research is their legacy." — Jeff Nielsen.

"The WBGA were everyday heroes who worked to improve the industry for barley farmers. They didn't seek the limelight or public attention. They focused on results — on marketing freedom." — Rick "Crash" Strankman.

"The changes we made were pretty damn good. I think we ended up with a better system." — Jack Gorr.

"One of my best recollections of my time with the WBGA was the opportunity for personal comradery of like-minded farmers. The friendships and memories have lasted well beyond my actual involvement. The CWB had to go and the WBGA played a key role in that outcome." — Tim Harvie.

"We always prioritized the best interests of farmers. We always had consistently rational, reasonable arguments for the cases we were making. We were not radicals as some might have portrayed us. We were just on the right side of change and what has happened since then bears that out." — Glen Goertzen.

"The WBGA didn't always lead initiatives but they were like the wheels on a wagon — critical to it's success, impossible to move forward without them. They did the heavy lifting on many topics and were indispensable in transitioning the farming industry from the horse and buggy era to the modern-day, highly efficient industry it has become." — Pat McCarthy.

"The WBGA brought an industry together that could have floundered and died without their efforts." — Alanna Hermanson.

"The directors of the WBGA were pioneers in the way to lobby government. They were consummate, thoughtful individuals who came at a problem with professionalism, positivity and a united voice. They offered solutions as an alternative to complaints and the results bear witness to their commitment." — Gerry Ritz.

"In looking back, two things come to mind. Firstly, the WBGA should be remembered for getting rid of the CWB. Although that wasn't their primary intent, in the end it was their most significant achievement. Secondly, the WBGA produced an exceptional compilation of industry studies and projects. They really did their homework and supported many important reviews and analytical overviews relating to important issues and opportunities. Sometimes they challenged current processes and on other occasions they investigated new ideas and concepts. They did a lot of important work for farmers. I can't help but think that the work done by members of WBGA has been a gift to Western Canadian farmers." — John De Pape.

"Certainly the WBGA helped remove the monopoly from the CWB and they were regularly on the right side of policy debates and positions. Younger farmers today might not know or understand that so telling this history is important. The WBGA has done a lot during their existence." — Phil de Kemp.

"The members of the WBGA raised the profile of barley performing a valuable contribution to the farming community. They made it known barley is important to farmers and feeders and delivered improvements to price transparency, a strong alternative for farmers and overall industry progress. They typify the western spirit of strong, independent free enterprisers." — Dave Guichon.

"They were a group of farmers who had a legitimate interest in the broader picture of agriculture. For them it was more than producing a crop. They developed the industry with a business approach." — Blair Louden.

"The WBGA was certainly the group that put the first chink in the CWB's armour. From there they just keep chipping away at the CWB. But I think what they should be remembered for is their role in making the market a better place for the next generation. They are the ones who will benefit from the work done by the WBGA." — Paul Cassidy.

"The farmers of the organization opened doors previously closed to farmers. They pre-dated the commissions and helped pave the way for a better future by taking policy discussions back to the farmer." — Brenda Brindle.

"Nobody could ever doubt the intentions of the people involved (in the WBGA) were all stellar." — Jay Burrows.

"The most obvious result of the efforts of the WBGA was the end of the CWB monopoly but, for me, the real accomplishment is lifting barley from being the weak sister to a profitable crop alternative. They put barley on the map." — Brian Rossnagel.

"The thing that was outstanding and memorable to me about the WBGA was the quality and strength of them as individuals and the contribution they made organizationally in a world that was very antagonistic towards them. They were always well prepared and reasonable people." — Al Loyns.

"They were shit disturbers. They saw some things that were wrong and they were quite willing to stir the pot to push forward with their beliefs." — Charlie Pearson.

"The WBGA had un unwavering fight for market choice. They never let go of that focus. "Give us the freedom to market our own grain."- Richard Phillips.

"There's no shame in being courageous about your position. The Barley Growers were a small group of farmers with a lot of credibility to their arguments and their position. They never gave up. It really was a David and Goliath situation." — Paul Orsak.

"The WBGA was a group of passionate, committed, innovative, brilliant farmers focused on change for the benefit of farmers and industry. Without their voice and effort we wouldn't be where we are. They were willing to risk it all for the benefit of all farmers. They were their own political movement." — Alanna Koch.

The legacy of the WBGA is a study in determination. The heart and soul of the WBGA was their belief in individual rights and freedoms. Their defining attribute was their persistence to secure those rights for themselves and those who follow in the proud tradition of Canadian farmers. New organizations could learn a lot from the history of the Western Barley Growers Association. They would be well served to follow in their visionary and accomplished footsteps.

A final tribute to any and all who played a part, either large or small, in the activities of the Western Barley Growers Association. Their results are testimony to what can be achieved by a small, dedicated and determined group of individuals. The road to success has been long and it was a helluva ride along the way.

This doesn't mean the work is done. New organizations representing and/or including farmers are much stronger now and better connected to the development of ag policy, regulations and the advancement of trade. All farmers are represented at the table and have a voice in their future thanks to the efforts of the WBGA and other farmer-led groups.

As a final thought, a quote from Dr. Emmett Brown in *Back to the Future* seems fitting here. He said, "Your future hasn't been written yet. No one's has. Your future is whatever you make it, so make it a good one."

Russ Crawford

APPENDIX 1

WBGA Board & Staff

Board

	1977	1978	1979	1980	1981	1982
President	Rick Thiessen	Lloyd Groeneveld	Hugh Craig	Hugh Craig	Fred Randle	Fred Randle
First VP		Rick Thiessen	Bill Lausen	Cal Ausenhuis	Cal Ausenhuis	Cal Ausenhuis
2 nd VP		Don Gibb	George Jackson	George Jackson	David Calderwood	Don McNeil
Secretary	Gerry Bakken					
Treasurer						
Past President	N/A	Rick Thiessen	Lloyd Groeneveld	Lloyd Groeneveld	Hugh Craig	Hugh Craig
Director	Brian Clarke	Bill Lausen	David Calderwood	David Calderwood	William Emrich	John Bevers
Director	Lloyd Groeneveld	Art McAllister	Art McAllister	William Emrich	William Hilz	William Hilz
Director	Tom Hyland	George Jackson	William Hilz	William Hilz	Gordon Reid	Gordon Reid
Director	George Jackson	Owen Harbicht	Owen Harbicht	Gordon Reid	Don Gibb	Rod Green
Director	Svend Jensen	Andy Toma	Don Gibb	Don Gibb	Bill Lausen	Stan Wiskel
Director	Gordon Kroon	Aubrey Milner	Aubrey Milner	Bill Lausen	Walter Tarapacki	Walter Tarapacki
Director	Kramer Ruppe	Tom Hyland	Walter Tarapacki	Walter Tarapacki	Francis Simpson	Romeo Lauzon
Director	Lindon Smith	Francis Simpson	Francis Simpson	Francis Simpson	Merle Layden	Merle Layden
Director		Bill Fulton	Larry McKee	Larry McKee	Pat McCarthy	Pat McCarthy
Director		Fred Randle	Fred Randle	Pat McCarthy	Ed McNally	Ed McNally
Director		Gerry Bakken	William Siegle	William Siegle	Don McNeil	Lindon Smith
Director		Don Wieben	Don Wieben	Don Wieben	Don Wieben	Herb Wall
Director		Gordon Adams				

	1983	1984	1985	1986	1987	1988
President	Gordon Reid	Don McNeil	Don McNeil	Tim Harvie	Tim Harvie	David Hueppelsheuser
First VP	Don McNeil	Tim Harvie	Tim Harvie	David Hueppelsheuser	David Hueppelsheuser	Richard Nordstrom
2 nd VP	Stan Wiskel	Stan Wiskel	Stan Wiskel	Glen Goertzen	Glen Goertzen	Jack Gorr
Secretary						
Treasurer		Merle Layden	Merle Layden	Peter Edgar	Peter Edgar	Ed Armstrong
Past President	Fred Randle	Gordon Reid	Gordon Reid	Don McNeil	Don McNeil	Tim Harvie
Director	Walter Abramski	Walter Abramski	Peter Edgar	Norman Daines	Ed Armstrong	Lionel Bird
Director	Cal Ausenhuis	Robert Carr	Robert Carr	Jack Gorr	Jack Gorr	Ted Cawkwell
Director	Norman Daines	Norman Daines	Norman Daines	Warren Hilz	Warren Hilz	Warren Hilz
Director	Rod Green	Jack Gorr	Jack Gorr	Gwen Jackson	Gwen Jackson	Eldon Massey
Director	Tim Harvie	David Hueppelsheuser	David Hueppelsheuser	Derwin Massey	Derwin Massey	Derwin Massey
Director	BJ Knott	BJ Knott	BJ Knott	BJ Knott	Gerry Elliott	Gerry Elliott
Director	Romeo Lauzon	Romeo Lauzon	Romeo Lauzon	John Ollerenshaw	John Ollerenshaw	Peter Edgar
Director	Merle Layden	Maurice Schayes	Maurice Schayes	Maurice Schayes	Maurice Schayes	Lee Erickson
Director	Pat McCarthy	David Wark	David Wark	Fred Witney	Fred Witney	Fred Witney
Director	Ed McNally	Ed McNally	Glen Goertzen	Richard Nordstrom	Richard Nordstrom	Glen Goertzen
Director	Lindon Smith	Lindon Smith	Lindon Smith		Garry Jones	Donna Graham
Director	Herb Wall		Richard Nordstrom		Jim Kumlin	Art McElroy

	1989	1990	1991	1992	1993	1994
President	David Hueppelsheuser	Richard Nordstrom	Richard Nordstrom	Ted Cawkwell	Ted Cawkwell	Wayne Kriz
Vice President	Richard Nordstrom	Peter Edgar	Peter Edgar	Wayne Kriz	Wayne Kriz	Art McElroy
Alberta VP	Peter Edgar	Lee Erickson	Lee Erickson	Art McElroy	Art McElroy	Doug Robertson
Saskatchewan VP	Gerry Elliott	Ted Cawkwell	Ted Cawkwell	Eldon Massey	Eldon Massey	Darwin Kells
Treasurer	Ed Armstrong	Wayne Layden	Wayne Layden	Wayne Layden	Wayne Layden	Eugene Boyko
Past President	Tim Harvie	David Hueppelsheuser	David Hueppelsheuser	Richard Nordstrom	Richard Nordstrom	Ted Cawkwell
Director	Lionel Bird	Lionel Bird	Lionel Bird	Eugene Boyko	Eugene Boyko	Bill Blake
Director	Ted Cawkwell	Jack Gorr	Ruth Gorr	Alanna Hermanson	Alanna Hermanson	Alanna Hermanson
Director	Warren Hilz	Doug Robertson	Doug Robertson	Doug Robertson	Doug Robertson	Wayne Iddings
Director	Eldon Massey	Eldon Massey	Roy Sparkes	Warren Hilz	Warren Hilz	Warren Hilz
Director	Derwin Massey	Roy Sparkes	Alex Hamilton	Roy Sparkes	Darwin Kells	Ken Vadnais
Director	Roy Sparkes	Neil Henderson		Brian Geck	Brian Geck	Brian Geck
Director	Neil Henderson	Art McElroy		Alex Hamilton	Alex Hamilton	Buck Spencer
Director	Lee Erickson	Alex Hamilton		Buck Spencer	Buck Spencer	Glen Goertzen
Director	Fred Witney	Wayne Kriz		Glen Goertzen	Glen Goertzen	
Director	Wayne Layden					
Director	Donna Graham					
Director	Art McElroy					
Director	Jack Gorr					

	1995	1996	1997	1998	1999	2000
President	Wayne Kriz	Wayne Kriz	Buck Spencer	Buck Spencer	Greg Rockafellow	Greg Rockafellow
Vice President	Buck Spencer	Buck Spencer	Greg Rockafellow	Greg Rockafellow	Leo Meyer	Leo Meyer
Alberta VP	Doug Robertson	Doug Robertson	Doug Robertson	Doug Robertson	Doug Robertson	Doug Robertson
Saskatchewan VP	Darwin Kells	Darwin Kells	Darwin Kells	Darwin Kells	Art Walde	Art Walde
Treasurer	Eugene Boyko	Eugene Boyko	Ted Cawkwell	Marvin Fowler	Marvin Fowler	Marvin Fowler
Past President	Ted Cawkwell	Ted Cawkwell	Wayne Kriz	Wayne Kriz	Buck Spencer	Buck Spencer
Director	Bill Blake	Alanna Hermanson	Alanna Hermanson	Wayne Iddings	Alanna Hermanson	Alanna Hermanson
Director	Alanna Hermanson	Wayne Iddings	Wayne Iddings	Art Walde	Darwin Kells	Darwin Kells
Director	Wayne Iddings	Warren Hilz	Warren Hilz	Ken Sackett	Ken Sackett	Ken Sackett
Director	Warren Hilz	Brian Geck	Brian Geck	Leo Meyer	Ed Armstrong	Ed Armstrong
Director	Ken Vadnais	Art Walde	Art Walde			Albert Wagner
Director	Brian Geck	Greg Rockafellow	Greg Rockafellow			
Director	Art Walde					
Director	Greg Rockafellow					

	2001	2002	2003	2004	2005	2006
President	Albert Wagner	Albert Wagner	Albert Wagner	Doug McBain	Doug McBain	Doug McBain
Vice President	Russell Larson	Russell Larson	Doug McBain	Jeff Nielsen	Jeff Nielsen	Jeff Nielsen
Alberta VP	Doug Robertson	Doug Robertson	Doug Robertson	Doug Robertson	Doug Robertson	Doug Robertson
Saskatchewan VP	Art Walde	Art Walde	ArtWalde	Art Walde	Art Walde	ArtWalde
Treasurer	Alanna Hermanson	Doug McBain	Rick Strankman	Rick Strankman	Rick Strankman	Rick Strankman
Past President	Greg Rockafellow	Greg Rockafellow	Greg Rockafellow	Albert Wagner	Albert Wagner	Albert Wagner
Director	Lionel Bird	Lionel Bird	Lionel Bird	Lionel Bird	Lionel Bird	Lionel Bird
Director	Doug McBain	Alanna Hermanson	Alanna Hermanson	Alanna Hermanson	Alanna Hermanson	Alanna Hermanson
Director	Ed Armstrong	Ed Armstrong	Ed Armstrong	Jim Ness	Gordon Reid	Gordon Reid
Director	Gordon Reid	Gordon Reid	Gordon Reid	Gordon Reid	Roy Sparkes	Roy Sparkes
Director	Roy Sparkes	Roy Sparkes	Roy Sparkes	Roy Sparkes	Buck Spencer	Buck Spencer
Director	Buck Spencer	Buck Spencer	Buck Spencer	Buck Spencer	Mel Stickland	Mel Stickland
Director	Ken Sackett (ABC Liaison)	Ken Sackett (ABC Liaison)	Mel Stickland	Mel Stickland	Greg Rockafellow	Ed Armstrong
Director		Mel Stickland	Jeff Nielsen	Greg Rockafellow		Tom Hewson
Director		Rick Strankman				

	2007	2008	2009	2010	2011	2012
President	Jeff Nielsen	Jeff Nielsen	Jeff Nielsen	Brian Otto	Brian Otto	Brian Otto
Vice President	Tom Hewson	Tom Hewson	Tom Hewson	Tom Hewson	Tom Hewson	Doug Robertson
Alberta VP	Doug Robertson	Doug Robertson	Doug Robertson	Doug Robertson	Doug Robertson	Rick Strankman
Saskatchewan VP	Art Walde	Art Walde	Art Walde	Art Walde	Art Walde	Jeff Nielsen
Treasurer	Rick Strankman	Rick Strankman	Rick Strankman	Rick Strankman	Rick Strankman	
Past President	Doug McBain	Doug McBain	Doug McBain	Jeff Nielsen	Jeff Nielsen	
Director	Lionel Bird	Lionel Bird	Lionel Bird	Martin Hall	Doug McBain	Doug McBain
Director	Alanna Hermanson	Alanna Hermanson	Alanna Hermanson	Doug McBain	Gordon Reid	Gordon Reid
Director	Gordon Reid	Gordon Reid	Gordon Reid	Gordon Reid	Buck Spencer	Buck Spencer
Director	Roy Sparkes	Roy Sparkes	Roy Sparkes	Buck Spencer	Mel Stickland	Mel Stickland
Director	Buck Spencer	Buck Spencer	Buck Spencer	Mel Stickland	Albert Wagner	Albert Wagner
Director	Mel Stickland	Mel Stickland	Mel Stickland	Albert Wagner		Tom Hewson
Director	Albert Wagner	Albert Wagner	Albert Wagner			Martin Hall

From 2012 to the present the Board of the WBGA has remained the same with Doug Robertson as President, John McBain as Vice President, Doug McBain as Treasurer and Brian Otto as Past President. There have been periodic WBGA Conventions while the activity of the organization has been minimal.

In addition to the opening of the market through the removal of the CWB monopoly, many of the target topics of the WBGA have been addressed or are being undertaken by other organizations such as the Alberta Barley Commission, Barley Council of Canada and Grain Growers of Canada.

The WBGA looks back on the previous decades in retrospect and feels a great sense of accomplishment and gratitude for all the efforts and results of farmer members, governments, industry and affiliates in elevating the barley industry in Canada.

Staff

WBGA Staff		
NAME	POSITION	PERIOD
Bob Nugent	Secretary-Manager	1977–1978
William Lipsey	Secretary-Manager	1978–1980
Iris Sedore	Manager	1981
Dorothy Pinchin	Executive Secretary	1982
Linda Lukenbill	Researcher-Secretary	1983–1987
Garth Cochran	Editor	1985–1992
Anne Schnieder	Secretary-Manager	1988–1991
Kathy Cooper	Secretary-Manager	1992–1999
Diane Savage	Secretary-Manager	2000–2018
Brittany Walker	Secretary-Manager	2018–2022

THE END

Made in the USA
Monee, IL
19 November 2022

1f2fc855-b3e2-402d-a642-90889b21f54fR01